WESTON FULTON
in TENNESSEE

Edison of the South

DEWAINE A. SPEAKS

THE
History
PRESS

Published by The History Press
Charleston, SC
www.historypress.com

First published 2021

ISBN 9781540250544

Library of Congress Control Number: 2021945861

Also by Dewaine Speaks:

East Tennessee in World War II
Historic Disasters of East Tennessee
Murder & Mayhem in East Tennessee
Preparing for International Travel

This work is dedicated to the tens of thousands of employees who, over the years, worked for the Fulton Sylphon Company, which was founded by Weston Fulton in the early 1900s in Knoxville, Tennessee. It is especially meant for the men and women who worked for the company during the war years (1941–45). Often working on secret projects that the public knew nothing about and realizing that much of the work being conducted at the Fulton plant was critical to the nation's war effort, the four thousand employees often worked extra-long sixteen-hour shifts seven days a week.

Many of those who were working double shifts were inexperienced women who quickly learned with on-the-job training and older men whom the armed forces considered too old to fight. The Fulton plant was not alone with this type of workforce but was a microcosm of wartime industrial plants across America.

This arrangement freed up young men and women across the country and enabled them to go to war. This previously untried group of workers was asked to produce vast amounts of materiel for sixteen million soldiers, sailors and airmen who were fighting in many parts of the world. Without the resolve and tenacity of this hastily put-together workforce, the war would likely have lasted much longer, and victory would have been much more difficult to achieve.

CONTENTS

Contents

FOREWORD

I can easily relate to the passion that Weston Fulton had for weather because of our career choices to become meteorologists, but I was humbled, amazed and inspired by his creativity and ingenuity for invention. From the first development of the seamless metal bellows (still in use today) to the creation of an automatic river gauge while working for the National Weather Bureau, he was an inventor, entrepreneur, teacher and leader who was well ahead of his time. His legacy is evident not just in Knoxville or even East Tennessee but rather across the world.

—*Ken Weathers, Meteorologist*

———————

A s a college student, I volunteered at Fulton High because I wanted experience in the classroom before I started graduate school. Immediately, I felt welcomed and included by both the teachers and students, and when I became an intern, I knew that I wanted to teach at Fulton. It was the best decision I have ever made. I teach English language learning (ELL), which is a class for students whose first language is not English. We have the highest population of ELL students in the county, and it has been so great to be a part of the growth and diversity in the school. I have learned so much from my students and their journeys have been incredibly inspiring. They are passionate, intelligent, hardworking and so accepting. After teaching there for five years, I know that Fulton is my home. I have loved working alongside the teachers and administration, who always put students first. Our motto is: "Enter to Learn, Go Forth to Serve," and I believe we, as a community, strive to emulate that every day at Fulton High School.

—*Rebecca Henry*

———◆———

Fulton High School's administration, teachers and staff helped mold my two brothers and me, as well as many other relatives. It was the first and only Knoxville high school to offer college prep courses, as well as vocational courses. Both of my brothers, Phil and Eddie Speeks, followed the radio broadcasting vocational path. They continued to build on those experiences over their careers.

I chose vocational office education (VOE) as my path. My junior and senior years consisted of two to three hours daily in Mrs. Smith's VOE class. She taught us advanced keyboarding skills on an electric typewriter; how to use a ten-key calculator (by touch); shorthand, business math and English; how to create business documents and print mimeograph stencils; and how to be successful in our dress and interviewing skills. Our class accepted work from the local business community, as well as from our teachers. These assignments offered us real-life, hands-on experiences. Upon graduation, we possessed the skills necessary to be successful in business. It was Mrs. Smith's influence that encouraged me to seek my certification as a business and marketing high school teacher. My Fulton High classmates gather monthly as we continue our journeys in life together and plan our fiftieth high school reunion.

—*Dana Howard*

———◆———

Technological progress depends on creative geniuses who recognize a need and conceive an innovative solution distinctly different from conventional approaches. Some of these innovators are well known, such as Eli Whitney, Thomas Edison and Alexander Graham Bell, but the vast majority of inventors are essentially anonymous to the general public. For example, most know that Edison invented the incandescent light bulb, but how many know who invented the LED bulb that is rapidly replacing Edison's prize? How about Velcro or the zipper, which are standards in our everyday life? Innovative breakthroughs are even more obscure if they are a component of larger instruments, as is the case with Fulton's bellows.

Weston Fulton's bellows are clearly vital to the functionality of many complex instruments that must adjust to drastic fluctuations in pressure and/or temperature. This is especially true in aerospace applications, where systems and subsystems must function between atmospheric pressure and those approaching a pure vacuum.

One of the most famous of these instruments is the Norden bombsight, which contributed to precise daylight bombing by the Allies during World War II. As an aerospace engineer, I participated in the design and development of the USAF F-111 fighter jet and the NASA Saturn, Apollo and Space Shuttle programs. I was completely unaware of the importance of bellows in making many of these subsystems functional. For instance, the expansion of bellows resulting from a pressure differential with the change in altitude was critical in activating parachutes for the pilot escape of the F-111.

Only after moving to Knoxville, Tennessee, did I learn of Weston Fulton and his invention of the seamless metal bellows, which had occurred over a century ago. Dewaine Speaks, the national sales manager with Robertshaw Controls Company (formerly Fulton Sylphon Company), enlightened me of their diverse value. This tool has become a standard throughout many industries to compensate for significant pressure changes and to dampen vibration.

Decades after I transitioned from aerospace to hydraulics and hydrology, I required the use of a bellows. Three colleagues and I invented a very sensitive flow meter that we manufactured and sold to measure the flow of groundwater in boreholes. To prevent the extreme change in pressure exerted on the steel exterior of the instrument from crushing the delicate internal circuit boards when lowered under several thousand feet of water, we resorted to a device that had been in use for a century: a version of Fulton's bellows.

It appears likely that the lifespan of Fulton's invention will exceed that of Edison's incandescent lightbulb.

—William R. Waldrop, PhD, PE

ACKNOWLEDGEMENTS

For their assistance in remembering stories, furnishing photographs and constantly offering encouragement, tremendous appreciation goes to the following people and organizations:

Jack E. Webb
Dr. Bill Waldrop
Marjorie Waldrop
Rebecca Henry
Dr. Ray Clift
Carol Clift
Earl Wells
Howard M. Samples
Louis Kennedy
Kim Pratt
Russell Mayes
Karen Sims
Wilburn Cate
David and Missy
    Speaks
Robert Bottoms
Al Verges
Jay Talley
Seth Smith

Cindy Webb
Teri Webb
Raymond Faulkner
Don Huddleston
Harry Bannon
Larry Price
Fulton Bellows
    Company
Leon Ridenour
Byron Joganich
Joe Yarnell
Jim Boyle
Jack Simerly
Mike Armstrong
Rob Speas
Dan and Carolyn
    Harrison
Jane Hunt
The Boeing Company

Susan Day
U.S. Air Force Museum
Eddie and Tracey
    Speeks
Kelly Marsh
Jim Otto
Linda Pearson
David Counts
Jim Hackworth
Jim Reed
Jerry Riggs
Eddie Willis
Kathy Todd
Ruth "Sunnye"
    Tiedemann
Martha Fulton Wells
Suzie and Jim Henry
Ken and Sonja
    Weathers

Robbie Bottoms
Worth Campbell
Sandra Campbell
Tommy Gibbons
Phil Scheuneman
U.S. Library of
  Congress
Robert Rovere
Gayle Temple
Nancy Webb
Taigh Ramey
Paul and Peggy Sliger
Ed Price
Robertshaw Controls
  Company

Roger Sikes
Ed Dexter
Debbie Thomas
Dr. Jon Rysewyk
Kimberly Wright
Terry Howell
Lena Coker
Martha and Graham
  Wells
Dane Owen
Knoxville News-Sentinel
NASA
Mike Prince
Knoxville News
Fred Chadwick

INTRODUCTION

When Weston Fulton arrived in Knoxville, Tennessee, on Christmas Day 1898, no one envisioned the affect his arrival would have on the city and eventually the world. He had been recently assigned as a meteorologist by the U.S. Weather Bureau to operate the Knoxville office, which was located on the campus of the University of Tennessee. While on campus, he worked part time as a university professor in addition to his duties with the weather bureau. He also took classes at the school, earning a master's degree in mechanical engineering.

Interestingly, his first invention was conceived to eliminate the drudgery of one of his tasks as a meteorologist. Every day, he was required to measure the fluctuation in the depth of the adjacent Tennessee River, a chore that required him to trudge up and down a steep hill to read a stationary scale attached to a bridge pier. Thinking there must be a better way to accomplish this task, he set about developing an instrument that would automatically measure the river depth and send the readings to his office at the top of the hill. His invention, the seamless metal bellows, allowed him to assemble a device that would provide the information he needed. This seamless metal bellows was the basis of hundreds of breakthrough devices that he would go on to invent and obtain patents for.

Being an inventor at the dawning of the twentieth century was exciting for Fulton. The Industrial Revolution was well underway, and technology was changing rapidly. Because of his numerous inventions and patent requests, the U.S. Patent Office dedicated a room solely for his applications, and the press began to call him the "Edison of the South."

Fulton's inventions were so successful that he opened a manufacturing facility to produce the thousands of metal bellows and assemblies needed to supply his needs, as well as the market for the many applications developed by other manufacturers. His company became one of the backbones of the Knoxville economy, expanding and employing several thousand individuals through the years.

As a successful businessman, Fulton was able to contribute to other aspects of life in Knoxville. In addition to his involvement in philanthropic and civic affairs, he joined other local business leaders in developing new industries, and he was elected to serve on Knoxville's city council and became the city's first vice-mayor.

Weston Fulton passed away in 1946, but his legacy lives on in a local high school that was named in his honor. Fulton High School was one of the first high schools in the South to offer dual technical and vocational courses along with traditional classes. Today, the company he founded continues to manufacture thousands of seamless metal bellows for domestic and international clients. The manufacturing methods used to make the bellows are very similar to those Fulton used more than a century ago.

1

THE FULTON FAMILY FACES A NEW REALITY

Weston Fulton was born on August 3, 1871, on his family's plantation near Tuscaloosa, Alabama. For decades, the Fulton family lived a somewhat idyllic life in the antebellum era of the old South. Their large plantation and its fertile soil provided bountiful harvests every year. Their plantation home, Farview, and their church, Bethel Presbyterian, were the centers of their social life.

This comfortable lifestyle suddenly ended with the outcome of the Civil War. Weston Fulton's father, William Frierson Fulton II, along with most young men in the South, joined the Confederate army and fought tenaciously in an attempt to hold on to the family's somewhat aristocratic life. During his time in the military, William kept a journal, and his writings provide a rare description of what plantation life had been like before it was changed forever. He also gave firsthand observances of the many Civil War battles he participated in.

At this time, many of the freed people were still feeling their way along as they tried to determine just how much better off they were then. This sudden, dramatic societal change brought about as much uncertainty for them as it did for their former owners. A few of the freed people actually stayed on the farms where they had worked for free and then worked for an hourly wage. Most, however, did not, and without their free labor and with the future uncertain for all, it would take several years for the economy of the South to recover.

Even though the inequities and cruelty of slavery had ended, the formerly enslaved were still left in a sort of "no-man's-land." There was no system in place to help them gain the benefits of citizenship, such as access to education, acknowledgement of their rights and opportunities in general that were afforded to the White population.

A federal agency called the Bureau of Refugees, Freedmen and Abandoned Lands, usually, referred to as the Freedmen's Bureau, was established by Congress in an attempt to help the newly freed individuals survive until they could find their way in their new and often complicated world. The agency was founded by President Abraham Lincoln in 1865 and terminated in 1872 by President Ulysses S. Grant. The bureau was poorly funded from its inception and was deeply resented by White southerners. It had some modest success in helping oversee some labor contracts between Black and White people and operating courts where employer-employee disputes could be resolved.

The dramatic changes of the previous few years meant that Weston Fulton would not enjoy the idyllic lifestyle that Fulton family members had experienced since 1735, when his ancestor David Fulton of Ulster, Scotland, received a royal grant from England's King George II for seven hundred acres of land in South Carolina. Financial success had come to the Fulton clan, and by the early 1800s, Fulton's grandfather William Frierson Fulton owned a large plantation and a large number of enslaved people just south of Tuscaloosa, Alabama. In 1865, like so many in the South, the Fulton family faced a new reality.

In his 1919 book, *Family Record and War Reminiscences*, Weston Fulton's father offers a rare firsthand description of the many Civil War battles in which he fought to preserve his family's status quo, and the book gives a view of what plantation life was like in the South prior to the Civil War. Much of the material in the remainder of this chapter comes from his book.

FOUR YEARS OF FUTILITY

The long, thin line of soldiers in tattered gray uniforms slowly marched through the early morning fog toward their designated place near Appomattox Court House, Virginia. With another long line of men dressed in blue silently observing the procession, the Army of Northern Virginia slowly stacked their arms and laid down their colors. The date that they would all remember forever was April 12, 1865, four years to the day after the war had begun. All present knew the South had lost the long and bloody war. Most suspected that for many of the Confederate soldiers, their lives would never be the same.

In three days, the Confederate soldiers would be paroled and set free to return home. A makeshift temporary camp was quickly completed, and the soldiers spent the three days reflecting on the past, and if they dared, they thought a little about the future. One of these soldiers was William Fulton, who, in six years, would become the father of Weston Fulton, a man whose inventions would affect much of mankind.

William had been a senior at Oglethorpe University in Georgia when Fort Sumter in Charleston, South Carolina, was fired on by Confederate troops on April 12, 1861. He raced back to Farview, his plantation home in Alabama, to join the Confederate army. He later wrote, "I reached home and found the war spirit aflame on every hand. Nothing else thought of or talked about. People seemed desperate, and many were anxious for it to commence, seeming to prefer the actual thing to the suspense that hung over the hearts of all."

Most southerners wanted and expected war to come. Some even feared the conflict would be over before they could get there. This was the general feeling when Fulton and his newly formed unit paraded in front of the American Hotel in Gainesville, Alabama. They then stood in line, he said, "with merry laughter and jest on their lips, all light-hearted, about to bid adieu to friends, relatives, and boyhood friends, and all that rendered life happy, many of them, alas, forever."

Fulton's unit, the Fifth Alabama Battalion, boarded a train for Manassas, Virginia. After several days on the train, with pretty girls showering them with flowers and friendliness at every stop, they reached their Virginia destination. Soldiers from other states were also arriving by train. William indicated that "most of these regiments were composed of fine-looking, stalwart men. All were full of enthusiasm for the fray."

Fulton's unit was ordered to Cock Pit Point on the Potomac River. By this time, winter had come for the poorly equipped rebels. At night, they posted pickets on sand bars in the river to prevent any landings by the enemy. William observed that "this picket duty was something never to be forgotten. The wind along and across the river had full sweep, as cold as the North Pole." Before Fulton's unit took part in the battle at Mechanicsville, Virginia, he was promoted from private to second lieutenant.

In rapid succession, the Fifth Alabama Battalion went on to fight in battles at Second Manassas, Harper's Ferry, Fredericksburg and Chancellorsville. Early morning light on July 1, 1863, found them in Gettysburg, Pennsylvania.

Day one of what would be a three-day battle went well for the Confederates and was generally regarded as a clear victory for them. One of the two units that were first in the battle was Lieutenant Fulton's Alabama battalion. The day ended after the Union forces were driven from the town of Gettysburg and onto the hills south of the town.

Fifty years later, William was still questioning why his commanders called off their pursuit when it was clear the enemy was on the run. "Why we failed to push on and occupy the heights around and beyond Gettysburg is one of the unsettled questions. Our army expected to do so and was disappointed when we did not."

The war would last almost two more years, but the inability of the Confederates to get reinforcements and ample provisions meant they could no longer fight the Union forces toe to toe. Lee's army slowly became encircled, and he surrendered his Army of Northern Virginia to General Ulysses S. Grant and his Army of the Potomac.

The number in Lee's depleted and demoralized army had been reduced to a meager twenty-seven thousand. When the Fifth Alabama Battalion was organized on May 5, 1861, it numbered around three hundred. The battered unit then surrendered just four officers and fifty-three enlisted men.

Lee's surrender essentially ended the war that had cost the lives of more than 600,000 Americans. While a total of 204,000 soldiers in both armies had died as a result of their battle injuries, incredibly, 414,000 died from diseases, such as cholera, dysentery and typhoid fever.

After the mandatory three days in the temporary camp, William Fulton and twenty other Alabama men started the weeks-long walk home. Sometimes, they were able to sleep in barns and corncribs. Some farmers shared their meager provisions with them. Along the way, no flowers were thrown, no admiring girls were to be seen.

Fulton returned briefly to the family's plantation, but the family soon moved to a much smaller farm. In his later years, William often traveled to Knoxville, Tennessee, to visit his son Weston Miller Fulton.

A Firsthand Description of Life on the Family's Plantation

The years just before the Civil War were a time of relative peace and quiet. It was similar to the proverbial lull before the storm, because the lives of millions of people were soon to be turned upside down. For others, this period led to a fledgling start on an uphill battle to freedom.

Because the enslaved people had worked hard under the hot Alabama sun, they developed a novel type of music that seemed to make their work a little easier and the days go by faster. A song leader would improvise some words, and as they called out their part, the rest would respond in concert with the chorus. The songs were inspiring, as the workers poured their hearts and souls into them.

William Fulton recalls playing with enslaved boys who were about his age:

As soon as quitting time came, the younger ones were merry as larks, and the boys of my age and size were ready with a game of marbles in the shade of the spreading oak. At nightfall, in the fall of the year, a 'possum hunt was always in order, and often have I roamed the woods at night with those Negro boys who had been hard at work the day previous, and yet, when the dog "treed" they would outrun me to get there first. At Christmastime, the neighborhood White boys would get a band of Negro boys, and all hands together would yoke up a string of yearlings, and such a time as we had breaking those calves to a yoke.

William remembered that "wedding days for slaves were reason for a holiday for Blacks and Whites. The frock worn by the young slave girl was often a dress that had been discarded by one of the White girls. Likewise, the suit worn by the groom was often recognized as a well-worn hand-me-down. None of this mattered, because all present had a grand time."

Clearly, seeing the advantages that go with having an education, the immediate priority of the newly freed people was obtaining access to the education system. They knew that without schooling, they would never be able to achieve equality. Former Union general Clinton Fisk, who had become an official with the Freedman's Bureau, reported in 1866 that Black people were "hungering and thirsting" for an education. He observed that "the colored people are far more zealous in the cause of education than the Whites. They will starve themselves and do without clothes, in order to send their children to school." Freed people eagerly went to work acquiring teachers and building schoolhouses.

As early as 1869, only four years after the end of the Civil War, a young Black girl in Nashville, Tennessee, demonstrated the results of her recent learning in an articulate note written to a northern mission, thanking them for their assistance. Eleven-year-old Alice Tompkins's complete note follows:

Kind friend:
This is the first time I have ever tried to write to any of our northern
friends. We have a pleasant school and good kind teachers and schoolmates.
I feel very much interested in our school. It is true I am very small, but
the small can do something. I want to be useful while I am young, and
when I grow up, I hope to make a useful woman. I am trying to serve
the Lord, who is so good and kind to all. I want to see the day when our
race will be educated. We are learning fast, and if we keep on, we will
be able to teach others.

A Time of Adjustment for All

In an attempt to comply with a federal law enacted by Congress in 1865, Weston Fulton's grandfather William Frierson Fulton proposed an agreement with his seven dozen enslaved people. The intent of the law was to help support the formerly enslaved until they could find their way in their new and confusing world. The agreement called for the formerly enslaved to receive, "as a further compensation, one-tenth of the wheat and one-sixth part of corn, fodder, potatoes, ground peas, and sorghum" grown on the plantation. They would also receive housing, food, clothing and medical attention as needed. As part of this short-term agreement, the formerly enslaved would continue working as they had previously from September 1865 until January 1, 1866, when the agreement would be ended. The agreement between Fulton and his former enslaved people was handwritten and discovered in his desk drawer in the former plantation house, Farview, 130 years after he had drawn it up.

The following list gives the names of the freed men, women and children who appeared on Fulton's proposed agreement:

Ben	Andrew	Raleigh	Mary
Hampton	Liva Ann	Felix	Jade
Chittie	Bilo	Gaeme	Circe
Wills	Salley	Mary	Fanney
Abe	Adline	Tick	Jimmie
Ike	Billie	Nancy	Emmaline
Jack	Hanna	Angie	Anarchy
Emily	John	Lydia	George
Lovis	Mart	Frank	Adam

Alp	Caroline	Charles	Joe
Lavinia	Sarah	Tim	Vina
Neva	Sam	Martha	Emma
Unnamed infant	Unnamed infant	John Henry	Daniel
Henry	Petter	Emeline	Mary
Julia	Lizzie	Leah	Leander
Alp	Henrietta	Maria	Sol
Johnnie	Celia	Unnamed infant	Lampe
Florence	Billie	Horace	Thebe
Jolen	Paffel	Lon	Lassie
Jim	Ellen	Eley	
Kate	Vira	Annie	

EDUCATION AND EARLY CAREER

Weston Fulton's mother, the former Mary Brown Hudson, died in 1882. The marriage between Mary and William produced Weston and his five siblings. During the following year, Fulton's father, William, married Mary Virginia Keene. William always called her "May," a nickname he gave her. His second marriage produced nine more children.

Until he was eighteen years old, Weston Fulton and his brothers worked in the fields of their farm. A staple crop each year was cotton. Because of the lingering depressed economy at the time, however, they were fortunate to receive five cents per pound for their cotton. Years later, Fulton was asked how he had been able to stand the hard work under the hot Alabama sun. His answer was, "I point out that it wasn't so bad—was much better than starving to death."

It might have been the hard work in the cotton fields in the sweltering Alabama sun or perhaps his inquiring mind that led Weston Fulton to leave the farm to attend the University of Mississippi in Oxford, Mississippi, and eventually work at and attend the University of Tennessee in Knoxville, Tennessee. Whatever it was, it did not surprise his large family or his friends. It was obvious to all that from an early age, Fulton's intelligence would enable him to escape the monotony of dragging his pick sack through the hot cotton fields on the family farm.

Initially, Weston attended Howard College (now Samford University). His uncle, however, was the chancellor at the University of Mississippi, so it was a natural move for him to transfer there, even though it was considerably farther from his home. He graduated in 1893 with a bachelor's in meteorology with highest honors, and he was valedictorian of his class.

Fulton spent the next five years working as a meteorologist at various weather stations in Vicksburg, Mississippi, and in New Orleans, Louisiana. His salary was sixty dollars per month. After moving to Louisiana, he began taking part-time graduate studies in mechanical engineering at Tulane University.

While working in Vicksburg, he met Marion Quinn, who later became his first wife. Surprisingly, Marion was about fifty years old, while Weston was only about twenty when they eloped to New Orleans. They were married there on February 25, 1895.

A woman marrying a much younger man was very unusual in the 1800s, but Marion had done it before when she married James Sherrard, who was eleven years her junior. That marriage lasted thirteen years, until James died at the young age of thirty-three. The couple had no children.

When Weston brought Marion (who preferred to be called Mary) to the farm in Alabama for a visit, it was obvious to all that she was a city girl and not at all comfortable in the country. Members of the family found it humorous that she could not tell the difference between cotton and okra.

Fulton's experience in the field of meteorology led him to accept an assignment as weather forecaster at the weather bureau station in Knoxville, Tennessee. The station had been moved to the University of Tennessee campus earlier that year at the request of then school president Charles Dabney. The United Sates Weather Bureau had only recently selected certain universities to train people who were interested in studying to be meteorologists, and Fulton was asked to set up the curriculum for that program.

2

A DESCRIPTION OF KNOXVILLE, TENNESSEE, UPON THE FULTONS' ARRIVAL

losely paralleling the Industrial Revolution, the discoveries that led to improved comfort and convenience for most people in the civilized world came in rapid succession. Knoxville, Tennessee, at the time the Fultons moved there, was caught up in these types of technological breakthroughs and rapid change. As industrialization proceeded, the state's cities experienced rapid growth. Initially, many of the jobs were held by farmers who worked only part time on public jobs while still maintaining their farms. Sometimes, wives worked in the textile mills while their husbands continued full-time work on their farms.

Although the economy of Tennessee trailed most of its northern neighboring states, the early 1900s saw the state slowly becoming more prosperous. The city of Knoxville, for instance, shared in this expansion of prosperity. The city was able to significantly extend its miles of paved streets and its system of trolley lines that had been electrified since 1890. People could then conveniently travel to all parts of the city. Regularly scheduled trains allowed Knoxville's citizens—and most people in Tennessee—to travel to distant destinations quickly, comfortably and inexpensively. Most people in the city were enjoying the recently available electricity, and homes with telephones were becoming more numerous. With the transportation system greatly improved and a new way of communicating over wire, friends and relatives in faraway places suddenly seemed to be much closer.

As the state of Tennessee and the South in general were caught up in rapid change, the economies of Knoxville and Chattanooga enjoyed the

City of Knoxville Fire Department, 1898. *Courtesy of Thompson Photo Products.*

benefits of the addition of several industries. The population of Knoxville continued to grow, especially when it was able to annex two adjacent small towns. At the turn of the century, its population was 32,637.

In the 1890s, Tennessee became a popular place to live and invest in for many former Union soldiers. By 1896, this had made Knoxville the third-largest wholesaling city in the South. Iron mills, cloth mills, machine shops and furniture factories flourished there.

If the Fultons had bought a newspaper on the day they moved to Knoxville, they would have read the *Journal-Tribune's* headline that reported, "Europe Swarms with American Agents." The lead article with a London, England byline lamented that the Americans were wresting much of the economic power from Great Britain. "It is not exaggeration to state that the former topic compelling attention in Europe, and in Great Britain in particular, is the remarkable, aggressive, commercial prosperity that the United States is manifesting." The article pointed out that this seemed to be on the minds of most Europeans, and few had failed to notice the giant strides that America was taking as it started moving into first place in the alignment of world powers. A leading London banker reportedly said, "This is the first time in

Soldiers returning from the Spanish-American War. *Courtesy of Thompson Photo Products.*

financial history that New York has been in a position to dictate money rates to London, Berlin and Paris."

While the last years of the nineteenth century brought many positive changes to Knoxville, sometimes, unwanted troubles also arose. In his book *Knoxville: This Prismatic City*, Jack Neely pointed out a couple examples of these problems.

THE BATTLE OF DEPOT STREET

In 1897, on Depot Street, two thousand Knoxville men were fighting for the right to be there. Some had shovels, some had fire hoses and some had warrants—one would lose his life.

The stage for the conflict was set a few years earlier. William McAdoo, a local attorney, owned Knoxville's mule-drawn streetcar system. In 1889, he built a revolutionary all-electric streetcar network—the first in the South. His new equipment was not durable enough, however, and broke down much more often than his previous mule-drawn streetcars. Faced with unusually heavy maintenance costs, McAdoo's modernized streetcar line was forced into bankruptcy.

When McAdoo moved to New York City, C.C. Howell assumed ownership of the bankrupt line, had the equipment repaired and made a success of the failed company. Despite this, in 1896, McAdoo returned to Knoxville to build a new competing line: Citizens Street Railway. Howell refused to allow McAdoo to lay streetcar tracks on Depot Street because he already had tracks there.

McAdoo, however, ordered his two hundred employees to dig up the street so he could lay his tracks, and when Howell's men arrived, a tremendous riot started. The city police arrived and arrested all of McAdoo's men. In turn, Knox County police officers arrested the city policemen. By the time the melee had ended, Knoxville's police chief and mayor were also under arrest. Surprisingly, the fight was broken up when city firemen showed up and turned their water hoses on the large crowd of brawling men, thus ending the "Battle of Depot Street."

Interestingly, after his colossal failure in Knoxville, where he had been jailed for inciting a riot, McAdoo recovered and went on to have an incredibly successful career. He was a planner of New York City's subway system, became secretary of the treasury, was the first chairman of the Federal Reserve and became a candidate for the presidency of the United States while he represented the state of California as its senator.

TERROR ON THE CABLE CAR ATTRACTION

In 1894, a cable car was to be installed that ran from the University of Tennessee side of the Tennessee River, 350 feet up to the top of Cherokee Bluff (still known as Longstreet Heights) on the opposite side. The Cherokee Bluff terminus of the cable car ride was at the location where the City of Knoxville was planning to build a public park. As advertised, riding the cable car that moved along the cables would offer a tremendous view of the city and surrounding area. It was said that the car and cables had been tested by running five tons of sand up and down the cable numerous times. The proposed ride and its uniqueness were written up in the technical magazine *Scientific American.* No one was sure if it was just an experiment or if it was a permanent tourist attraction. The *Knoxville Tribune* reported, "It is said to be the only passenger car of the kind in the world. Such cars have been used for freight in Europe, but none for passengers so far as known."

The cable car had been operating only a few months when, on an unseasonably warm Sunday afternoon in late February 1894, a large crowd of Knoxvillians eagerly waited in line for their turn to ride the new attraction. On the ride's first run of the day, six men, a woman and a teenage boy got into the gondola. The engines started, and the cable car moved smoothly on its thirty-degree trajectory upward, higher and higher above the surface of the moving water. Astonishingly, two car lengths from the top of the bluff, the passengers and the operator heard a loud cracking noise. To some, it sounded like an explosion. Investigators would always be puzzled by the many different descriptions of the sound that the snapping of the pulling wire made. Nonetheless, it had snapped, and the car started careening with horrifying speed back down the twin cables. Operator T.C. Lewis immediately tried to apply the cable car brakes, but they had no effect on the plunging car.

Suddenly, the dangling pulling wire whipped across the car and became tangled around the car and the main cables. This caused the out-of-control car to come to a sudden, violent stop. The passengers were thrown on top of one another in the lower end of the car. The eight passengers and the operator of the car were then dangling 135 feet above the flowing Tennessee River. One passenger was restrained from jumping from the car by the other passengers. While most were in need of immediate medical attention, young attorney Oliver Ledgerwood, who was hit in the head by the broken cable, was dying.

Hundreds of horrified people, who soon gathered on both sides of the river, had no idea how to rescue the trapped passengers. No one had ever been stranded above a river in a cable car before. In a frantic attempt to try something—not knowing if it might be of any help—witnesses on Cherokee Bluff fastened a rope to one of the cables and let it slide down to the car.

Coincidentally, at the same time, a steam-powered yacht called the *Vollet* was returning from a Sunday afternoon excursion to the Lyons View area of west Knoxville. The captain could see that a disaster was occurring and carefully maneuvered his boat directly under the stranded car. The captain was able to maintain his position in the flowing water while the stranded passengers devised a makeshift sling from the rope that had been lowered to them. Then, one by one, they lowered themselves by rope down to the yacht. The crowd cheered each time a person was lowered to the safety of the boat. Eventually, only the unconscious Ledgerwood remained in the car.

Next, a man on shore named Andy Harris volunteered to attempt to reach Ledgerwood. He was taken to the boat, and with what the onlookers described as super-human strength, he climbed the 135 feet to the cable car. He entered the car, hugged the unconscious man to his body and descended the rope to the waiting yacht. This incredible act of strength and heroism, however, could not save the life of the young lawyer. Oliver Ledgerwood died two hours later.

A coroner's inquest was held to investigate the death of thirty-two-year-old Ledgerwood and to determine the cause of the horrible incident. Investigators were alarmed to learn that the pulling wire had been intentionally partially severed. An engineer for the cable company, George W. Keller, gave intriguing information. He testified that his examination revealed that two of the three strands "had been cut either by a cold chisel or had been beaten in two, leaving the third strand to operate the car." It was Keller's opinion that the cable had been cut on the Cherokee Bluff side by "parties not desiring to have the cable in operation." He told the investigators that there had been other attempts to sabotage the operation. He said that on one occasion, rocks had been placed in the gears that were used to propel the car and "had to be removed before the car could be operated."

After several days, the cable car company was assigned the blame—not for having defective equipment, but for being careless in not protecting the apparatus against sabotage. The coroner said, "We believe the accident was due to the carelessness of the owners in not guarding or protecting the cable that had been tampered with on several occasions." With this brief time in operation, Knoxville's distinctive attraction passed into history.

KNOXVILLE'S MARKET HOUSE

In many ways, one of Knoxville's main meeting places, the Market House was unusual. According to writer Jack Neely, its uniqueness may have lain in its diversity. Not only were several skin colors represented there but many dialects, both domestic and foreign, could be heard. Many of the farmers not only produced the fruits and vegetables sold there, but they also owned their own stalls and shops. Tourists and poets made remarks about them—sometimes with a smirk but often with a kind of awe. Among the Market House's diverse customers were ladies with parasols who sent their children to private schools, summered in New York and often had a chauffeur waiting for them at the southern entrance.

3

FULTON THE METEOROLOGIST

Weston Fulton was asked to present a paper at a convention of weather bureau officials in Omaha, Nebraska, on October 13 and 14, 1898. His paper and accompanying talk were titled "Effect of Forest Clearing and Cultivation Upon: First, Water Supply and Soil; Second, Rainfall; Third, Temperature."

One section of the paper compared rainfall that falls on a forest to that which falls on an open field:

> *A portion of the raindrops which fall upon the forest will be intercepted by the foliage of the trees, and the water thus collected will run down the twigs to the branches and thence down the trunk of the tree to the ground. The rain, therefore, which falls upon the forest will be fed to the nearest water course by the slow process of underground drainage, and the water course which thus receives its supply from the forest will maintain a comparatively even flow and will not be subject to sudden and violent overflows.*

Fulton went on to explain that the first rain that falls on the open field packs the soil and retards percolation and filtration. "Excess water then rushes down the slopes carrying soil with it." He told the group of meteorologists that the soil that has been carried down by the water will sink to the bottom and begin filling the stream. "Soon after the rain has ceased to fall, the water supply will become exhausted, and the flow of the water course will be reduced to the opposite extreme."

Ever the ecologist, Fulton told his peers at that 1898 convention that protecting the environment was one of their most important tasks. "We are to account to coming generations for the progress made in this age along this line. Let us then, each and all, be up and doing."

While working at the Knoxville Weather Station, Fulton taught meteorology at the University of Tennessee and took courses himself as he worked toward a master's degree in mechanical engineering. He completed the required courses and received a master's degree in 1902.

Fulton was a charter member of the University of Tennessee chapter of the Phi Kappa Phi Scholarship Fraternity. At that time, a group of three universities took a small fraternity to the national level. These schools were Pennsylvania State University, the University of Maine and the University of Tennessee.

Because of the Greek courses he had taken at the University of Mississippi, Fulton would have known that the organization's motto, "Philosophia krateito photon," meant, "Let the love of learning rule humanity." The fraternity's first home was the University of Maine. This prestigious fraternity is currently headquartered at Louisiana State University in Baton Rouge, Louisiana.

As weather observer in charge of the U.S. Weather Observatory in Knoxville, Fulton was responsible for the local work being done by the government as it investigated the meteorological conditions of the upper atmosphere with box kites. In particular, he was interested in determining how much air expanded when lightning passed through it. For this experiment, he was going to need a piece of equipment that did not exist at the time.

The results of his observations were published as a part of a collection of scientific articles issued by the University of Tennessee between 1899 and 1902. A few years later, the data collected from these experiments became important in the training of observers who furnished weather reports for the network of airlines that was beginning to operate between cities all over the United States.

As part of his meteorological duties, Fulton was expected to go to the Tennessee River each day to record the fluctuations in the level of the river. Gauging the amount of water, especially during times of heavy rain, was critical in the flood-prone Tennessee Valley prior to the construction of the Tennessee Valley Authority dams. This job had always been done by his predecessors by going to the river and checking a large-scale board that hung vertically from a bridge pier.

These daily trips to the river called for Fulton to trudge down and back up a part of the University of Tennessee campus known locally as "the Hill."

This daily chore caused him to look for a method to measure the slightest variations in the river's depth and send the readings automatically to his office that was located at the top of the hill. Coincidentally, the device needed to meet this challenge was similar to the one he needed to help measure the expansion of air when lightning passed through it.

After weeks of experimentation, Fulton developed an instrument that he hoped would solve both problems. The device was a small metal tube with corrugated walls—the first flexible metal bellows. The seams of the walls of his first bellows burst under stress. However, he soon perfected a method of producing an engineered seamless metal bellows from drawn brass tubes, thus eliminating the troubling seams in the bellows. On November 21, 1901, the weatherman-turned-inventor, filed for a patent on his new seamless bellows. He named it "sylph" after a word created by Paracelsus, a German-Swiss scientist in the 1500s, to describe mystical beings in the air. His initial patent was assigned no. 729,927.

Fortunately, the bellows sensor in the bottom of the river was not disturbed by passing boats or other wave action. The recording instrument in his office could record several days of data. The U.S. Weather Bureau immediately saw the potential of the device and bought several bellows assemblies from the young inventor and installed them in other river locations. The instrument became so popular that the U.S. government helped Fulton promote it and published a pamphlet titled *The Fulton Automatic River Gauge*.

After his initial patent for his seamless metal bellows, the "Edison of the South," as Fulton came to be called, sent so many patent applications to the United States Patent Office that it set aside a room dedicated solely to his patent requests. The March 31, 2007 edition of Ireland's *Ulster-Belfast News Letter* reported that "Weston Fulton, known as 'the Edison of the South' was not a man to fritter away time." An article in the December 5, 1989 edition of the *Knoxville Journal* stated, "Fulton was a prolific inventor, sometimes called Knoxville's Thomas Edison."

In the 1900 census, Fulton's wife, Marion, conveniently subtracted fifteen years from her age. She indicated that she had been born on September 1860 instead of September 1845. Weston listed his correct age, but in an attempt to look a little older, he grew a beard.

In September 1908, Marion returned to Vicksburg, Mississippi, alone. She was sick and knew she was dying, so she moved in with her half-sister Julia Quinn Geary. Marion died on November 3, 1908, when she was sixty-three years old. Her obituary in the *Vicksburg Evening Post* stated that she was leaving behind "her devoted husband, Weston Miller Fulton of Knoxville." Surprisingly, from that day on, Fulton would not speak of her again and did not want anyone else to mention her. The family never learned the reason for this self-imposed silence.

Two years later, Fulton was issued a passport. The passport application indicated that he was thirty-eight years old and stood five feet, six inches tall. His eyes were blue, and his hair was black. He indicated that he would be making a trip and returning within six months.

On August 17, 1910, Fulton married Barbara Stuart Murrian, whom he had met through mutual friends while

Weston and Barbara Fulton. *Courtesy of Fulton Family Collection.*

attending a dance. She was nineteen years old, and he was thirty-eight. No longer needing to look older, Fulton shaved off his moustache and beard. A few days after the wedding, the newlyweds sailed for Europe. This was a combined honeymoon and business trip as Fulton investigated marketing opportunities for his bellows in Europe.

Weston and Barbara had five children: Weston Miller Jr., Barbara Alexander, Robert William, Jean Hudson and Mary Helen. Their oldest child, Weston Jr., called "Buddy" by the family, was said to have shared his father's fascination with technology from a very early age. The Fultons had two employees: Rosa English, their cook, and Maybelle Webster, the family nurse.

All of Fulton's inventions were not of a serious nature—some were almost whimsical. For instance, the driveway in front of the Fultons' home, located near the University of Tennessee campus, was short, and backing out into traffic was sometimes difficult. Because of this, Fulton designed and built a turntable on his driveway, on which he could turn his car around and drive forward into traffic. He built and patented a bellows-powered steam engine that he took to trade shows to advertise the bellows's versatility. (The engine can still be built per the original drawings.) The clock that hung on his office wall was no ordinary clock, as it needed no winding. As the temperature of the day changed, the thermosensitive charge in the bellows alternately boiled and condensed, automatically winding the clock. It was covered by a patent labeled "winding mechanism for clocks."

Fulton was active in local philanthropic and civil affairs, and like so many industrialists of medium-sized towns, he also entered politics. In 1923, he was elected to Knoxville's city council and was chosen as the city's first vice-mayor. He was part of a slate of candidates elected during the city's transition from a commissioner-style government (which had been accused of corruption) to a council-manager form of government. Fulton was instrumental in the city's hiring of a particular city manager who unfortunately proved to be controversial and was ousted after one term. After this experience, Fulton never ran for office again and advised his children to avoid politics. Regarding his four years in politics, he said somewhat humorously, "They nailed me to the wall."

4

A NEIGHBOR'S CHANCE REMARK

Fulton's engineered seamless metal bellows were the beginning of a long string of inventions and resultant products that were developed using his inventions. His educational background and his intimate knowledge of weather conditions led him to devote special study to the recording and regulation of temperatures. His discovery of new principles and devices in that field had so much obvious commercial importance that he severed his relationship with the United States Weather Bureau after he had taken a one-year leave of absence to conduct his special studies. Giving up his career in meteorology, he then devoted all of his time and efforts to being an inventor, manufacturer and entrepreneur.

A chance remark by a neighborhood steamfitter who was visiting Fulton as he worked in his woodshed caused Fulton to give serious thought to the application of his bellows for controlling the damper on furnaces, thereby enabling the wintertime temperature in homes and offices to be automatically controlled. The steamfitter said, "There is a fortune waiting for anyone who can apply your bellows as an automatic damper regulator on furnaces in homes."

The patent that Fulton had been granted back in 1901 was for a sealed bellows filled with a volatile liquid that could be used in hot water heating systems. Its operation was simple. When heated water in the furnace boiler caused the volatile liquid within the bellows to boil, this boiling liquid gave off gases that expanded the bellows, which, in turn, closed the draft, thereby checking the fire. As the water temperature fell, the bellows contracted much like a spring, pulling the damper open again. A variation of the same regulator could also be used to control steam heating systems.

Fulton had already developed the needed device that the steamfitter described and had an approved patent on it. This simple sounding, yet significant bellows application would allow the masses to automatically and comfortably control the temperature in their homes and offices. This device became the first of many products to be sold in large quantities. The steamfitter's advice had been sound.

Fulton could readily see the almost limitless applications for his invention, but his capital had become exhausted, so he sought financial backing from some of his friends. John S. Brown and P.J. Briscoe provided investment funds for his venture.

In the fall of 1904, Fulton and Brown united as the two executive officers of the Fulton Company. They were soon able to move from the cramped laboratory and workshop that Fulton had maintained in his garage to the top story of a two-story brick building near the University of Tennessee. This property, in 1982, would become the site of the Saudi Arabia exhibit on Knoxville's World's Fair grounds.

With adequate space to work in, Fulton was able to procure and install the laboratory equipment he needed to build prototypes and test his ideas much faster. Working models, drawings and inventions came at a startling rate. Unfettered by space limitations, his chief constraint became a lack

Assembly department employees. *Courtesy of Kelly Marsh.*

Fulton (*in vest*) and employees, 1906. *Courtesy of Jerry Riggs.*

of time. His work became his hobby and entertainment. What started as a small business on the second floor of a machine shop began to grow as engineers and scientists from around the world found applications for Fulton's "sylph."

In 1914, a new manufacturing facility at 2318 Kingston Pike, about one and a half miles west of downtown Knoxville, was completed. Obtaining property next to the University of Tennessee campus seemed appropriate, given the many ties Fulton had to the school.

THE ENGINEER'S FRIEND

The bellows had so many practical applications in instruments, engines, gauges, switches and thermostats of all kinds that it is difficult to completely comprehend the magnitude of what Fulton created. The bellows was far from an ordinary tube with corrugations. His bellows became so important to industry that the word *sylph* and the Fulton-created word *sylphon* became well known in the engineering world.

A repeatable spring rate, a known burst pressure, a calculated life expectancy and its availability in almost all metals made the bellows an engineered core for many types of instruments in the days long before computers. Importantly, the bellows would return to its original shape if it had not been overstressed, and with these benefits, it quickly became a mainstay for the manufacturers of pneumatic temperature and pressure controllers and recorders.

Since Fulton's earliest products solved lingering problems for engineers in most parts of the world, his business grew rapidly as he almost invariably furnished prototypes for his prospective customers to test.

The following are some examples of early applications for bellows.

- The performance of high-voltage electrical contacts is improved when the contacts are sealed inside an evacuated chamber. Sparks are largely eliminated by evacuating the air from the contact area. Dangerous sparks become more manageable and controllable. A bellows can be soldered or brazed to one contact and to the housing, which allows a vacuum seal to be maintained around the contact. The flexibility of the bellows allows the free movement of the contact to make or break the circuit.

- Bellows are used to seal between the body of a valve and its rising stem. Dangerous, odoriferous and cancer-causing chemicals can leak from valves when their typical rubber or plastic packing rings are worn. To solve this problem, a bellows can be brazed or welded to the valve stem and to the valve body. The flexible bellows, therefore, allows the valve stem to move inside the bellows while maintaining a leak-proof seal. In modern times, the advent of the computer chip has brought about a need for a valve that will be able to seal out any foreign particles that might contaminate highly sensitive manufacturing processes. Hundreds of thousands of stainless-steel bellows are currently being used as leak-proof seals in this application.

- When a pressure gauge is measuring very low pressures, bellows can be used instead of conventional bourdon tubes. The much more sensitive bellows easily detect the very low pressure changes and give a more accurate reading than bourdon tubes.

- Because of Fulton's background in meteorology, a natural application of his bellows was to sense barometric pressure. The bellows was evacuated of air and sealed. The resultant movement of the bellows gave an indication of barometric pressure on an integral dial. The development of aviation presented a new application for the bellows. Because of the correlation between barometric pressure and altitude, a version of the barometer was put into immediate use on aircraft. It was then called an altimeter for this application.

- Using this same approach, bellows were used on both aircraft and automotive engines as fuel controls. The bellows sensed the barometric pressure and adjusted for the air-to-fuel ratio to adapt to the changes between the heavier air at low altitudes and the lighter air at high altitudes.

- When automobiles started being produced by the millions, they all required a thermostat in their cooling systems. Bellows were the sensing devices on the early automobile thermostats. The bellows had a liquid charge that consisted of a mixture of methyl alcohol and water. As the vapor inside the bellows expanded with the increasing heat, it forced the valve stem to move, thereby opening the valve. The liquid-charged bellows would automatically open or close the valve sufficiently to maintain the desired temperature. However, because the bellows are sensitive to changes in pressure as well as temperature, and since the coolant system of modern-day automobiles is pressurized, bellows are no longer used in automobile thermostats.

GROWING PAINS FOR HIS YOUNG COMPANY

Many inventions and products flowed from Fulton's fertile mind during the next several years, but it was the bellows and products that contained bellows that offered the most potential for his company. As with any organization, the Fulton Company had its share of challenging times. Fulton, the company's president in 1922, told the company's directors that their sales organization was "demoralized and lukewarm." He was also particularly concerned about the many competitors that were beginning to make metal bellows, as his customers did not appear to hold a strong loyalty to his firm. He also saw problems appearing due to rapid employee turnover and reported discord among some of the workers.

He went on to tell the directors that some of these problems had been resolved by hiring a new general manager. He praised his chief engineer, who worked during a time when his department was being slowed down by "special investigations conducted for us by our patent attorney." He said that despite the hindrances, "the engineering group created several new designs, developed numerous new tool drawings and completed over three hundred special orders." He proudly pronounced that this was "all accomplished at a total expenditure, including salaries and overhead, of $15,918.66."

At the turn of the century, Fulton's ideas and products were new, and in the eyes of some, untested. Because of this uncertainty, many prospective customers were initially reluctant to try his products. This changed, however, in 1905, when he signed a contract with the world's largest distributor of heating appliances. American Radiator Company became the exclusive sales agent for the distribution of bellows that were to be used in steam-related applications.

Under the contract, the radiator company agreed to start an aggressive sales campaign that included a vigorous advertising program. This campaign soon brought Fulton's name to prominence and helped reinforce the validity of his patents and made it less likely—or so it was thought—that other manufacturers would attempt to make similar bellows.

After fifteen years of a mutually beneficial relationship, serious friction developed between the two companies. By 1920, it had become obvious that the relationship could no longer continue. The conflict likely came from a decision by the American Radiator Company to begin manufacturing bellows in direct conflict with the Fulton Company.

The Fulton Company's history recorded: "This unfortunate turn of affairs brought the Fulton Company face to face with a serious crisis." The company had not only lost its sales agent and, at the same time, most important customer, but then it also had a formidable competitor. To make things worse, the radiator company's decision to question the validity of Fulton's patents encouraged others to start infringing on his patents. The Bishop and Babcock Company of Cleveland, Ohio, also began manufacturing bellows in direct violation of the patents. Rayfield Carburetor Company, located in Chicago, and Janesville Laboratories quickly joined in and started making bellows.

Fortunately for Fulton, he had the foresight back in 1907 to patent not only his bellows but also the very processes that he had developed in order to

Above: The making of a bellows. *Courtesy of Jerry Riggs.*

Left: Fulton's most important invention, the seamless metal bellows. *Courtesy of Jerry Riggs.*

make the bellows. These patents became extremely important, as the Fulton Company was then fighting for its very existence. The company's recorded history reveals:

> *In self-protection, the Fulton Company was compelled to embark upon a campaign of expensive litigation against the infringers. The task of building up a sales organization to replace that of the American Radiator Company, while carrying on costly patent litigation in the face of rapidly growing competition, was most discouraging... The outlook for the company was at its lowest ebb.*

A new sales force was established, and new markets were sought. It was decided by Fulton that he would defend his patents, and litigation was started against the infringers. Fulton personally testified for hours in each of the two lawsuits he initiated.

Several months later, on February 13, 1925, a sweeping decision in favor of the Fulton Company against the Bishop and Babcock Company was rendered by Judge D.C. Westenhaver, district judge of the Northern District of Ohio. Following this ruling, on March 31, 1925, a similar decision was handed down against Janesville Laboratories. These favorable, though very expensive, decisions brought with them public confidence in the validity of Fulton's patents and served as a powerful deterrent against further infringements.

More good news came from the newly established sales group, as it once again started getting positive results. The struggling company was getting back on its feet. In 1925, bellows production was back in full swing and would continue for approximately another seventy years.

By January 1927, the value of the company had grown to $6 million. There were 7,500 outstanding shares of stock that were valued at $800 each.

5

WORLD WAR I

The war that started on July 28, 1914, and ended on November 11, 1918, would eventually be called World War I. It is estimated that about 8 million soldiers and sailors died during the war. Even though the United States participated in the war for only seven months, it suffered 117,000 deaths, with more than 200,000 injured.

Several new types of warfare were introduced during this war. Chemical weapons were used for the first time. Although they were still in their infancy, airplanes were used to drop bombs on ground troops. Machine guns were able to fire 600 rounds per minute—the equivalent firepower of about 1,500 rifles of the types that were being used at the time. Because of the large numbers of submarines that were used by several different countries, underwater bombs, or depth charges, were developed to counter the threat they posed.

Early in the war, German submarines were sinking large numbers of British military and commercial ships. This caused Great Britain to hurriedly develop and manufacture depth charges. These consisted of a canister that was filled with explosives and rolled off the stern of a ship. The kill ratio was low because the explosive had to detonate within about thirty feet of the submarine to penetrate the hull, which was heavily reinforced to withstand the tremendous pressure that is exerted by the sea.

The British ship RMS *Lusitania*, on May 7, 1915, was sunk by German U-boat *U-20*, and 1,198 passengers, including 123 Americans, lost their lives. The ship was just eleven miles off the southern coast of Ireland and sank within eighteen minutes. The sinking of several other civilian ships ended any delusions that the "civilized" manners of nineteenth century warfare could survive into the twentieth century.

The outrage Americans felt as a result of this incident made it easier, two years later, for President Woodrow Wilson to get approval to declare war on Germany. After an intercepted telegram indicated that the Germans were attempting to persuade Mexico to enter the war against Britain with the promise that they would help take back Texas, Arizona and California from the Americans, the United States' entry into the war was inevitable. On April 6, 1917, the American Congress voted to declare war on Germany.

Leaders in the U.S. Navy had realized for some time that a better defense was needed against the German submarines, which were being rapidly improved. Initially, the submarines could travel only about 300 miles from their base. By the time America entered the conflict, however, German submarines could routinely travel 2,500 miles and, with help from supply ships, were known to venture 10,000 miles from their home port.

The Americans realized that depth charges dropped at random had little effect on enemy submarines. To be effective, it was necessary for the depth charge to reach a depth comparable to that of the enemy submarine before detonating.

In 1917, American military leaders convinced the government of Great Britain to share its secret drawings and specifications for its depth charges, which were better than anything the Americans had at the time. In addition to the depth charge technology that had been furnished to them by Great Britain, U.S. Navy personnel still searched for ways to make that unit better.

For several years, the Fulton Bellows Company had been furnishing products for use by the navy. As is customary with all sizable navy contracts, inspectors regularly visited the company. During one of the routine inspections, Fulton told navy personnel that he had read in the newspaper about the alarming number of ships being lost to German submarines. The inspectors listened intently when Fulton told them, "I have something that might help—a little invention that might cut our losses."

When high-ranking navy officials heard of Fulton's idea, navy engineers started making regular visits to Fulton's manufacturing plant in Knoxville, Tennessee. It was a learning process for the navy engineers and for Fulton as well. Since his staff was relatively small, Fulton personally worked on the design of dozens of prototypes that he produced for the navy to evaluate. After many meetings and countless changes that were required by the navy, a successful product that had an impact on the outcome of the war was produced.

U.S. Navy torpedo boat. *Courtesy of the Maritime Park Association.*

The improved version of the depth charge that was developed used a hydrostatic "pistol" to detonate the charge like the original British unit. In the improved version, the depth charge's sheet metal canister was filled with explosives and a firing device. A tube passed through the canister from end to end. In one end of the tube was a small amount of TNT, which triggered the main explosives. The canister also had a safety pin and a cover. When the depth charge was launched, the safety fork and the cover were knocked off, allowing water to enter the canister. At a depth of about fifteen feet, the water pressure was sufficient to extend one of Fulton's bellows, which tripped a release mechanism. The "pistol" mechanism also contained a bellows, into which water entered as the depth charge descended. When the water pressure on that bellows reached a preset depth, the pressure released a spring that drove the firing pin into a detonator, setting off the full load of TNT.

With the addition of Fulton's bellows, the unit was safer to handle and much more accurate. A pattern of depth charges set at varying depths, usually fired two at a time, could be dropped just above the enemy submarine's location. It was said at the time that Fulton was responsible for sinking more

German U-boats than any other man. The navy never reported a single failure of Fulton's products. However, Fulton, a man who was said to have had a good sense of humor, joked after the war that this was a good business to be in, because if his products failed, it would still end up on the ocean bottom, and he would never have any returned material. A fact that was not released for years by the United States government was that some of the components in the depth charge that Fulton helped develop could be used to a depth of three hundred feet and were used in other military weapons that remained classified for years.

Fulton recalled several years after the war that the War Department representatives who came to Knoxville to meet with him in 1917 were initially wary of him. He thought they suspected that he was just another owner of a small company who was looking for a lucrative government contract. He said that he reassured the government representatives, "It's a simple thing that I have in mind. It's already tested in other uses. It's a device that could be installed on an underwater bomb. It would be hurled from the decks of destroyers and other ships to sink enemy submarines."

The success of the invention Fulton offered to the navy was described in Vic Weal's column in the *Knoxville Journal* from April 8, 1982. He pointed out that a "peaceful invention adapted to sea war hastened armistice. Fulton's gadget doomed the enemy submarine fleet." With the end of the war, Fulton turned his energy and that of his rapidly growing manufacturing facility to making peacetime products.

RECONSTRUCTED COPY OF FULTON'S 1917 WARTIME LETTER TO HIS FATHER

Dear Papa:

I have just gotten back from a trip to Washington and New York, and this will explain the cause of my delay in writing. Dr. Wilmer told Barbara two years ago when he fixed her eyes for her that she would have to come back again next spring and have her eyes tested again, and my eyes have been bothering me a little also, so we left here on the 1ˢᵗ and went to Washington and New York, where I had some things to look after.

I left trouble behind me and have had plenty since I got back. The rapidly advancing cost of living, together with the decided advances in wages which have necessarily followed have pretty thoroughly demoralized the laboring classes, particularly that class known as "organized labor." It is difficult to get anybody to work nowadays. The whole attitude is one of indifference and independence. Wherever the proprietor of a business is inclined to be a little energetic himself, he finds it quite exasperating to be constantly up against the indifference and often actual antagonism of most of the laboring element. I have been getting my full share of it for some time past, and am looking for it to continue until a return of "hard times," which I believe will gradually come on as the war is over, and within a year after peace is declared, I believe we will have a tremendous number of people out of work, and then the whole atmosphere will be full of the usual howl about hard times being brought on by "the moneyed interests" and all of the other kinds of fake political issues that accompany business depressions. If there were some way to make an accurate photograph of the attitude of a lot of these people now and reproduce these photographs when the depression comes, public opinion would be a good deal less sympathetic with the great mass of "unemployed" who will be clamoring for sympathy. Human nature is certainly a curious thing, but when we think of the ignorance of the masses of people and begin to realize how imperfect their understanding of the great problems of political economy is, there is little wonder that they are so easily led off after the alluring theory of trying to get "something for nothing."

Well, we are finally at war with Germany. Of course, I am thoroughly mad at the German government; I think President Wilson has finally done the right thing; I am right with him and have volunteered my services to the country for whatever duties it may be seen proper to put on me. I feel that we should fight to the finish and am ready to do my part. There is, however, one thing that mitigates slightly the offence which the German government has committed against us, viz: it has forced us to wake up and begin making the necessary preparation to enable us to take care of ourselves after the war is over. I have always thought that we were in no danger as long as those people in Europe were engaged in fighting one another, but I feared for what might happen to us when they got their differences settled so that they were footloose to do with us as they might wish. Of course, the pacifists argued that all of the present belligerents would be so exhausted that they would not bother us, but I never felt sure of that. Now that we have actually gone to work to get ready, I feel that all danger is past, provided the war lasts long enough for us to get on our feet a little, which I think will be the case.

Hoping this will find all hands well, and with love from us all,
Affectionately,
Weston

48

6

THIS EXPANDING AGE

An acquaintance of Weston Fulton, F. Romer, gives us a glance back to 1928 with his extensive contemporary writings, which illustrate in the flowery language of that era the tremendous effect that Fulton's inventions had on mankind up to that point. Some of Romer's 1928 insightful observations follow:

> *Here you are in the age of comfort. You demand in this expanding age, a constant expansion of your privileges. You are cluttered with comforts that a potentate of a hundred years ago would have regarded as special miracles of God. You sit in a soft chair, under light softened by a mellowing shade, enfolded by a soft-woven dressing gown, and you read to your wife, who wears a gorgeous colored frock, the news you get without effort almost the hour it's happening. You are called to dinner, and your menu is expanded by variety in food only possible because it may be variably temperated with electricity on the stove or refrigerator. You are made comfortable through a degree of house warmth thermostatically fixed without exertion on your part.*
>
> *All this expansion in all these directions greatly hinges upon a little expanding device which might never have been created if nature, by some freak whim occasionally noticeable in her, had discontinued thunderstorms before the year 1899. The comforts that you enjoy are so completely available only because W.M. Fulton, weather forecaster for Knoxville, Tennessee, was curious to know how much the atmosphere expands when lightning passes through it.*

Let a simple fact be stated. Air is gas and vapor. When lightning electrifies the two, they repel each other; the atmosphere expands. With this knowledge, the Knoxville weather forecaster set about making a contrivance in which gas and vapor might be sealed, and their expansion measured by the extended size of the container when an electric current passed through it. My father used to say, "Many things are settled in the woodshed." That's where W.M. Fulton took his problem and whipped it into shape. In an old woodshed back of his house, he commenced his experiments. For weeks, his family saw him only at meals—and many of those were missed. Mysterious hammering, grinding and other less identifiable sounds, like early saxophone practice, emanated from the woodshed. This is what really was happening: A flexible piece of metal was curved into a tube. Its edges were soldered. Then strange tools were patterned by the resourceful pencil of this inventive college professor who forecast the weather and something more important. A local machinist built the tools. He then corrugated and contracted the tube 'til it would limberly expand itself if an expanding vapor was formed in it by heat evaporating the water it contained.

He hooked the little bellows to a steam heating boiler. When the steam pressure rose, the bellows expanded, closed the draft and checked the fire. A great heating company at once gave the inventor a ten-year contract for all he could produce of the Fulton seamless metal bellows.

W.M. Fulton works standing up at the draftsman's board, where he gets his ideas on paper as fast as pencil will fly. "I'm the only man never without a pencil. I carry mine on a shoelace fastened with a safety pin on the inside of my pocket. A pencil's presence accounts for many developments in the use of the sylphon."

It seems a far cry from the comfort of that chair in which you sit to this little heat-regulating device. But the wood frame that gives your chair its commodious back and its arms their luxurious sweep was probably shaped in water which is steam-infused and temperature controlled by a sylphon bellows. Your soft light, your newspaper, and the brilliant color in your wife's frock, like a thousand other expansions of privilege, possession and pleasure, all trace their availability, economy of perfection to the expanding sylphon bellows.

Industry is humming the song of service in a voice vibrantly pitched by the little sylphon seamless metal bellows. In a place that spins and weaves cloth, hundreds of thousands of threads move on spindles and looms. A slight variation in temperature here would cause the threads, worked under a known tension, to break, and either ruin woven goods or hold up weaving. The Fulton sylphon temperature regulator maintains a fixed indication on *the thermometer in countless mills like that one. The dyes are made fast by temperature control when the cloth is immersed. The cloth is bleached before dying in vats temperature controlled by the sylphon bellows. The air in the drying machines is warmed at unvarying temperature so the operation may be timed—and a busy sylphon metal bellows regulates the warmth in these dryers. You can now comprehend what the Fulton sylphon has to do with the dress of your wife or the lounging robe you wear as you read to her.*

The glue on the stamps stuck to the letters mailed from the skyscrapers of commerce is made in kettles on which the Fulton sylphon perches, a watchful monitor. Some of these letters carry orders to industry by air mail. The airplanes reach their landing points safely, no matter how they bank, turn and dip, for the gasoline is fed to the motor at equal pressure in all altitudes at all angles by a sylphon seamless metal bellows operated as a pump by a moving part of the motor.

In creosoting shingles, preparing the chemicals for artistic roofing, at the kilns where fine brick is made, lumber dried, or tile glazing is done, and in the pigment dryers where your house paint is prepared, the expansions of the sylphon help to expand the modernized home comforts of America.

On the restaurant steam table, a busy bellows watches the thermometer. In the huge electric refrigerator, another tells the motor when to start and stop, just as it does in ice machines for the home.

Your table and canning sugar was produced with the aid of the Fulton sylphon metal bellows. You drink safe milk because a Fulton sylphon maintains the pasteurizer at its 143 degrees for the time necessary to secure the desired health standard. Your cocoa, spices and many other cooking ingredients are ground in rooms kept chill by this same little expander of life's benefits in providing the last of the three great needs—food, clothing, and shelter—the Fulton sylphon continues its expanding influence on the age.

After giving the address of a florist to his chauffeur, a man steps into a limousine. The silent motor is kept at the temperature best for powerful performance by a Fulton sylphon. It opens and closes a valve, regulating the water circulation around the motor, or moves a shutter on the radiator. From the florist, he purchases a beautiful bouquet of flowers that bloomed to rare loveliness in a greenhouse where the Fulton sylphon furnished the climate.

And so it was that we discovered you, perhaps a few hours after your call at the florist, seated in a soft chair, under light softened by a mellowing shade, enfolded by a soft-woven dressing gown, reading to your wife, who wears a gorgeous-colored frock, the news you get without effort almost the hour of its happening. The scent of the flowers fills the room with tribute to the Fulton sylphon and the part it plays in this expanding age.

7

TRAGEDY STRIKES WHILE A MANSION IS BEING BUILT

By 1929, Fulton had become a millionaire many times over and could afford luxuries most people never can. Perhaps it was this wealth that contributed to the event that is every parent's worst nightmare. Weston Miller Fulton Jr. (nicknamed "Buddy" by his father) had just turned seventeen when he entered the University of Tennessee as a freshman. Several of his friends, few of whom had access to automobiles of any kind, admired Buddy's new Packard convertible, and they were constantly asking for permission to drive it.

When Buddy and his friends found that the school cafeteria at Strong Hall had closed, they decided to go elsewhere for lunch. With one of his friends from New York driving and Buddy riding in the back seat, they drove west on Knoxville's Kingston Pike. Others who were riding in the car reported that they were initially going only about forty miles per hour. The driver, however, became impatient behind a slow-moving truck and decided to pass it. The driver lost control of the car and smashed directly into a utility pole. No one in the car was injured except for Buddy, who suffered a traumatic head injury.

For the next twelve days, the boy's fifty-eight-year-old father stayed by the critically injured patient's bedside at Fort Sanders Hospital. A *Knoxville News-Sentinel* reporter at the time said he found it remarkable that a "few blocks from the hospital, the vast Fulton plant continues to turn out by the thousands the Fulton products which virtually every civilized country will use. But Mr. Fulton is oblivious to all that humming activity as he sits by the bedside to catch the slightest move of his injured son." The boy died from his head injuries and meningitis at 9:40 p.m. on January 20, 1929, his grieving father at his side.

Fulton's dream house, 1940. *Courtesy of the Fulton Family Collection.*

Long before Buddy's death, the Fultons had started planning for a new mansion to be built in West Knoxville on Lyons View Drive. They had visited Europe and had admired the grand mansions and villas there. Fulton had taken his plans to local architect Charlie Barber, who, along with his cousin David West and Benjamin McMurry, had concentrated mostly on designing houses for the affluent clients in the upscale Sequoyah Hills community of Knoxville.

Charlie Barber was one of the South's most highly regarded architects, familiar with the Beaux-Arts and Gothic styles, but he was incredulous when he looked over Fulton's hand-drawn design. Barber quickly pointed out several areas in the design that would cause major problems to construct. Fulton was not swayed and insisted that it could be done and that this was the way he wanted his mansion to look.

Many years later, when Barber was an old man, he indicated that the design had been pulled in several directions because of all of Fulton's changes. The design had been well along when Fulton decided he wanted a ballroom on the third floor. This change brought about the need for an elevator, which, in turn, required a tower, completely changing the style of the house. Drawings for the gatehouse that are currently archived at Barber

Remaining arched corridors of Westcliff. *Author's collection.*

and McMurry Company, dated January 23, 1929, show the gatehouse as it was built. Drawings for the house itself, dated May 16, 1929, however, are different in several ways from the house that was ultimately built. Photographs indicate that several changes were made even after the mansion was completed.

The exterior walls of the opulent mansion were covered in Crab Orchard stone on the lower levels, with the upper levels covered with stucco. A service wing was located to the east of an axial corridor that began on the northern end. A dining room with windows that faced a courtyard was located on the eastern side of the house. Beyond the dining room was an impressively decorated main stairway. Eastward from an octagonal space was an arcade that formed the south side of the courtyard.

Six bedrooms with tiled baths, several dressing rooms and servants' quarters were located on the second floor. The shower doors in each of the bathrooms were made of leaded glass. Fulton used one of the bedrooms that overlooked the courtyard as his study. The large ballroom was located on the third floor and could be reached by the elevator or a stairway. Lavatories and a serving room were available for parties.

The gatehouse at Westcliff. *Author's collection.*

The office building inside Westcliff grounds. *Author's collection.*

A portion of the wall that surrounded Westcliff. *Author's collection.*

A roof garden could be reached by the elevator or a spiral stairway in a tower at the south side of the house. In addition to the garden, the tile roof supported a large gazebo. The interior halls led to octagonal lobbies. Roman-like arched galleries were on the south and west sides of the house. A domed roof with blue and gold tiles was the prominent feature of the house. The tower provided spectacular views in all directions, and a possibly true rumor circulated for years that said, from the tower, Fulton could see the grave site of his son across the valley in Highland Memorial Cemetery.

On the walls of several of the rooms are patterns that, from a distance, appear to be wallpaper. Upon closer examination, however, it became apparent that it was not wallpaper at all. The painted patterns were, in fact, created by artisans Fulton had brought from Europe to decorate the walls.

The swimming pool at the mansion, complete with regulation diving boards, was so spacious that the University of Tennessee used it for its most important swim meets during the late 1930s and 1940s.

Working through several heated arguments and design changes that Fulton kept proposing, Barber finished the construction of the magnificent mansion that was Fulton's dream house. When the mansion

A crab orchard stone wall in front of Westcliff. *Author's collection.*

The house donated to the University of Tennessee. *Author's collection.*

was completed, the Fultons moved from their house near the University of Tennessee's campus into their new home at 4275 Lyons View Pike in West Knoxville. It was said that Barber never considered Fulton's mansion one of his best efforts.

To memorialize the life of their young son, the Fultons donated their former home to the university. The house was used for more than eighty years as the school's health clinic and was officially called the Weston Fulton Jr. Memorial Infirmary.

8

MAKING PLANS AND NEW OWNERS

Through the years, the Fulton Company established and maintained an employee base that was loyal to the traditions of its founder. Ed Hooper, in the book *Knoxville* (Images of America), pointed out that because representatives of the U.S. government came to the company so often to have their problems solved, the company became known as the "can-do company." During the 1920s, Fulton began to heavily diversify the product line that his company offered and continued to improve the company's facilities and expand its capabilities. All of this made the company more attractive and, consequently, more valuable as he started thinking of selling it.

In 1930, when the bottom line was showing optimum profit—and with the onset of the Great Depression—Fulton sold his company. Because of his foresight in diversifying its product line, the Fulton Company rode out the Depression in reasonably good shape. Several years later, the company newsletter, the *Fultonews*, reported that despite the ensuing depression of the 1930s, the Fulton Sylphon Company, compared to other companies, actually prospered. Many Knoxvillians remember the company as a strong economic force in east Tennessee during the turbulent Depression of the 1930s.

After selling his company, Fulton's contact with the new owners usually came when they had questions or asked for his opinion. He said, "I drop by there frequently for a chat and drop a little advice when it's asked

Above: Company manufacturing facility, 1940s. *Courtesy of Kelly Marsh.*

Opposite: Pouring molten metal in a foundry, 1936. *Courtesy of Kelly Marsh.*

for." Several of Fulton's "boys" from the old days became managers of the plant and often sought his opinion on running the business. Fulton's brother Frank stayed on with the company as a production manager for another fifteen years.

The immediate goal of the new owners was to continue Fulton's plan of developing a more diverse product line. At that time, most of the products still featured bellows as part of their working mechanism. Developing products like special valves, level controls, pressure gauges and numerous automotive-related controls gave the company a diverse line that enabled it to fare well, even during the frequent economic downturns.

The new owner was Reynolds Metals Company, which had also recently purchased Grayson Controls Company and Bridgeport Thermostat Company. Grayson Controls immediately started purchasing Fulton Company's bellows by the thousands for use in the room thermostats it manufactured. Bridgeport Thermostat Company started buying bellows in large numbers for use in its automobile thermostats.

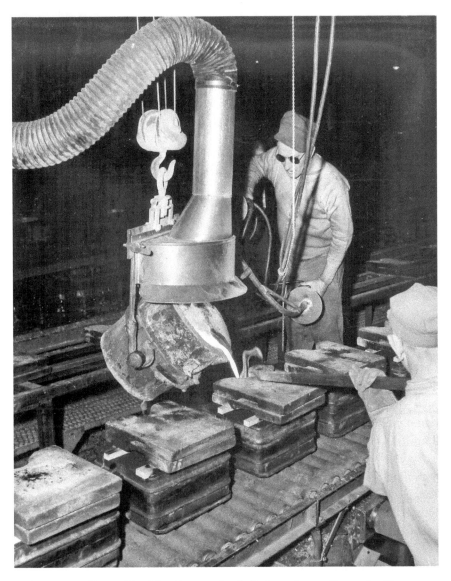

In 1947, Reynolds Metals acquired Robertshaw Controls Company and placed the Reynolds-owned firms that manufactured controls under Robertshaw Controls's leadership. The Fulton Company's name was changed to Robertshaw-Fulton Controls Company. Then in 1962, largely for the sake of convenience, the Fulton name was discontinued by the parent company, and the Knoxville plant became the Fulton Sylphon Division of Robertshaw Controls Company. In the 1980s, its name was changed to the Tennessee Division of Robertshaw Controls Company. Because of the many

Company machinist, 1942. *Courtesy of Kelly Marsh.*

name changes, for the remainder of this work, the company that Fulton founded will be called "the company."

Shortly before he made the surprise announcement that he was selling the company, Fulton bought a Knoxville manufacturing company called W.J. Savage, which specialized in flour mill and marble processing machinery. Fulton; his wife, Barbara; and other investors paid W.J. Savage, the company's founder, $250,000. Announcing the purchase, Fulton said, "It will be the policy of the new owners to continue the business in its present name and along the same lines as hitherto."

After the sale of the company, Fulton quickly acquired interests in several other local factories and businesses. These included the furniture manufacturer Royal Manufacturing and Tennessee Odin Insurance Company. The latter would be moved to a location on the western corner of Fulton's estate on Lyons View Pike. The office building, situated on three acres of land, was built of Crab Orchard stone and stucco. The building, with exterior decor that matches the mansion, is located a few hundred feet west of the mansion's gatehouse and is still in use.

With the company sold, most observers thought that Fulton wanted to dabble in these smaller companies mostly to occupy his still-fertile mind. In a few years, however, he gave the opportunity to each of his children to choose one of his companies to own and operate. His daughter Jean and her husband, James C. Talley, already owned a major manufacturing facility and did not need to accept the offer.

After his other children took responsibility for the companies they chose, Fulton had more time available and was free to do what he wanted. He immediately tackled the challenge of cleaning up the smoke-filled environment by developing a cleaner-burning coal-fired furnace, and as he worked, he applied for numerous patents. In many respects, it was the old days all over again.

TRAVELING WITH HIS FAMILY

A May 16, 1946 article in the *Knoxville News-Sentinel* reported that Fulton was a family man who enjoyed traveling with his wife and children. The article stated, "This they have done extensively, covering a greater portion of the world." Weston and Barbara had gone to Europe on their honeymoon in 1910.

In 1934, Fulton took his entire family to Europe, where they particularly enjoyed England and Switzerland. Even then, Hitler's Germany was in chaos, and the relatives back home worried that the family might be in danger because of Fulton's role in the development of the depth charge that was used so effectively against German World War I submarines. An October 12, 1934 *Knoxville News-Sentinel* article described in detail the German portion of the Fultons' trip. The reporter, Bob Cunningham, noted that during World War I, the name of the inventor was not given great publicity. Despite this, Fulton was not sure he could travel through Germany without being identified.

In the newspaper article, Fulton said humorously:

> *About the only secrets we had left after we got out of Germany were the secrets of our minds. Never saw anything like it. When we got to the Dutch–German border, men of the German Intelligence Service literally lined up beside us. The first one asked us for all literature and letters, and we opened up our baggage and our pockets to them, gave them all the papers, magazines, letters, or printing we had about us. Next, an intelligence man*

came and asked for our passports. Of course, we were used to that. The third man asked us for all of our money. We shelled it all out to him, paper and coin, and all letters of credit we had. He not only looked at it carefully, but he listed it all, the amount in coin, paper, letters of credit, and all the rest. These intelligence men speak English very well. With me were Mrs. Fulton, our four children and a nurse.

Having got these matters fixed up, we wanted to take a drive. The hotel furnished us two nice cars, and we started. We knew we were to have guides, but we didn't know we were to have those intelligence service men again. But they went with us, and they sure gave us an earful of Hitler's merits as a ruler. We noticed, too, that if we pulled out anything to read, one or both of these intelligence service men would read it, too. They would peep at our reading material over our shoulders. I know from our experience that Hitler's censorship system is rigid, and his control must be very complete.

The Fultons saw signs all over the country that said, "Those who are faithful to us will have jobs, something to eat and shelter." Several people back in America were relieved when the family sailed from Le Havre, France, for New York, on August 30, 1934, aboard the SS *Manhattan*. They arrived in the Port of New York on September 6.

After their trip, Fulton indicated that he liked the budgetary system of the British. In particular, he liked their manner of handling indigent and unemployed people. He said that they had unemployment benefits before the United States did, and they began their dole system before the United States began providing relief. Speaking somewhat prophetically, he said, "The British are doing relief and balancing their budget. We are doing our relief financing but failing to balance our budget. The sooner we treat it as a permanent problem and arrange to finance it accordingly, the better off we'll be."

ROUND-ROBIN LETTERS

In the days before electronic messages, and when long-distance telephone calls were very expensive, the Fulton family had a unique way of keeping in touch. Round-robin letters were in constant use. The dictionary describes this manner of communicating as "a letter that is circulated from person to person in a group with individual comments being added by each."

This means of communication became important with Fulton and his fourteen siblings, as the extended family grew large and was scattered over several states. While the news was not always timely, using this method of communicating ensured that everyone could generally keep up with things such as weddings, deaths, graduations and births. Surviving letters reflect the eagerness that family members often showed as they waited for the "robin" to return.

Dozens of these letters have been preserved. When the extended family gathers for its biannual Fulton family reunion, it has become a tradition for different family members to read several of the letters aloud to the group. This offers a glimpse back to a different time and helps keep the family close while preserving some history.

The following is a sample of a round-robin letter. Weston Fulton's father, William Frierson Fulton, tells Weston's brother Brown about seeing his first automobile and rationalizes that his family is better off without his former wealth. (Di is William's sister).

Larimore, Alabama, 11-29-1899

Dear Brown:

The robin finds me somewhat out of shape to meet its demands this time. I stumbled over a plank in the doorway this morning and fell against Di, and in her efforts to uphold me, she stuck her finger in my eye, and you know how that is, especially to one of my age....I did want to say a good deal about that trip to the Birmingham Fair that you boys might know how much I appreciate your kindness....Di wrote to Weston and Graham and told them she thought the "Mexican Band" was the biggest thing she saw, but that automobile carriage was my biggest. I have lived to see it. I saw a man driving his carriage about with perfect ease, turning, backing and propelling it forward, moving slow or fast, and there was nothing but the four wheels and body—no tongue or horse. Well, it was worth the trip to see it.

The property I owned at Woodlawn is now worth half a million dollars. Suppose I owned it now? You boys would soon be "no account." You would quit work, dress fine, part your hair in the middle and be mean to your wives. It's a good thing that it's just as it is. You wouldn't have the opportunity to send Di and me out on these sweet, delightful trips either.

Di wrote to Weston about my taking her and Neva into the "Midway." Well, we didn't tarry there long. Birmingham is on a boom, a substantial business boom. Everybody seems to be at work, and if he is idle, it's his own fault. In my short absence, I can note many remarkable changes for the better.

Now, something of home, and I will close. We keep well—our crops are all out and housed. My wheat is up and is a nice stand and looks fine.

All hands join me in love to you and Neva, and we are going to keep the latch string on the outside wall until after Christmas anyway—so you must both come.

W.F.F.

9

WITH WAR APPROACHING, THE FAMOUS NORDEN BOMBSIGHT EMERGES

Even though he no longer owned the company, Fulton's personal reputation and the company's reputation were still indelibly linked. U.S. Navy personnel remembered Fulton's contributions during the Great War, and when storm clouds were gathering again between 1936 and 1940, Fulton's former company was one of the factories identified by the navy to produce goods if war did come. When Germany invaded Poland in 1939, the government's military readiness panel stepped up its number of visits to the company. Engineers, chemists and other technical personnel were already in place. The facility had its own foundry, plating shop, fully equipped machine shop, qualified quality control personnel, a small lot department for manufacturing engineered samples quickly and a full-time registered nurse.

By the 1930s, the design of aircraft had become sophisticated. From the materials used on their skins to the navigational instrumentation in their cockpits, airplanes were starting to resemble the aircraft of today. Built by manufacturers like General Electric Company, Allison Company and Pratt and Whitney Company, their engines had become more powerful and more reliable. Heating systems for flying at very high altitudes were a few years away, but planes were being fitted with oxygen to enable crews to fly altitudes over forty thousand feet.

Even with these innovations, the U.S. Army Air Corps still had a pressing need. For several years, its engineers had searched for something that would enable their bombers to accurately drop their bombs. With bombing runs ranging between 220 and 250 miles per hour, knowing when and where to release the bombs was critical if the target was to be hit. Complicating matters, the bombs, when released, tended to follow their host plane before pitching down at a more vertical attitude. The trajectory of a falling bomb tends to form a geometric parabola. Making things even more difficult, at the time, no one had previously accurately calculated the trajectory of bombs that were often falling at speeds greater than the speed of sound, which, at sea level, is about 768 miles per hour.

With appropriated money to spend, the air corps began working with several inventors who were attempting to come up with an acceptable bombsight. Carl Norden, a Swiss inventor, received a government contract and, in 1930, furnished several thousand of his bombsights to the air corps. The army, however, decided that it needed something better. Thinking that Norden was on the right track, the air corps funded more of his work.

In an effort to make his bombsights more accurate and more user-friendly for the bombardiers, Norden began consulting with engineers at the Fulton Company. Norden's new design incorporated six bellows assemblies on each of his bombsights, which compensated for such variables as changing airspeed and altitude. Drift, because of side winds, as well as the weight

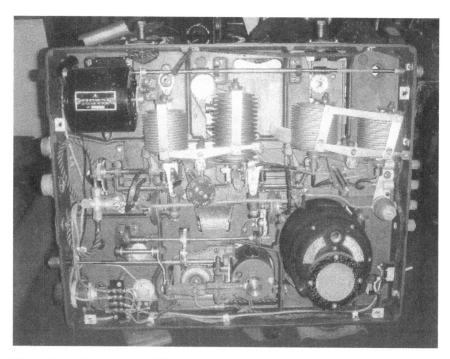

Norden bombsight. *Courtesy of Taigh Ramey, www.TwinBeech.com.*

of the ordnance being carried were also part of the equation. In essence, Norden, in collaboration with engineers of the company, had developed an analog computer before the age of computers.

As the bomber was nearing its target, the bombardier entered in the air speed, altitude, wind direction, expected drift and data on the ordnance that would be dropped. Once the target was identified, the bombardier would actually assume directional control of the aircraft through the bombsight, which was connected to the autopilot. The Norden bombsight, using a system of internal sensing devices, including the six Fulton bellows and stabilizer controls, automatically released the bombs. The bombardier called out "bombs away" as the aircraft lurched upward with the release of its heavy load.

During the war that would indeed come, the following are recorded instructions from an excited bombardier to his pilot and fellow crew members in the frantic moments as they neared their target, dropped their bombs, and then headed home:

> *Target ahead...about fifteen degrees left...maybe six miles....Watch that formation....Stay in there tight, and when I call for level, that's what I mean, quick....Watch toward the sun for fighters....Lead group is going in now.*
>
> *Top turret! Fighter at eleven o'clock our level....They look like FW-190s....Get him! Now, flak closer, start evasive action. Here he comes— top turret! Come on, hit him.....Nice shooting, think you got him!*

As they reached the point where the bombardier took control of the aircraft, the bombardier continued:

> *Give me level, George....Start the camera, Beezy....Hold it level....Watch the airspeed....Bomb bay doors open....Steady, steady, just a little longer now....Level, level, hold her level...steady....Bombs away! Let's get the h—— out of here!*
>
> *Flak on the other side now....There goes a fortress out of formation ahead....Bomb bay doors closed...camera off, Beezy. Boy, the eggs were right in there, gang, swell bombing...Look at the smoke down there.... What a mess!*
>
> *Take over, George, and take her home!*

The bombsight was a rather primitive computer—although not primitive for the time—but it helped shorten the war. With more precision, there were fewer sorties flown, and the amount of collateral damage was reduced. Supposedly, the use of the bombsight made it possible to drop bombs within a thirty-foot circle from an altitude of four miles.

Albert Pardini wrote the following in his book *The Legendary Norden Bombsight*:

> *The Norden bombsight was born in the 1920s, involving fundamental and applied research, such as unprecedented bombsight engineering, design, complex mathematics, unheard-of machining of metal parts to tolerances of one thousandth of an inch...on massed produced parts manufactured to watch-like measurements, development of precision anti-friction ball bearings, optical equipment refined to new tolerances, and the industrial ability to produce delicate instruments in mass quantities never before attempted. All of this was accomplished long before the discovery of high-speed computers, calculators, and the event of the micro chip. This was a testimony to the ability of the American complex to react to a very critical time during the first part of* [World War II].

Norden's bombsight had more than two thousand manufactured parts, and the government paid him $8,800 each for the ninety thousand bombsights his company manufactured. The company furnished bellows for twenty thousand of these bombsights. Norden's profit was approximately 10 percent, and his company ranked forty-sixth among industries in the number of wartime contracts received during the war.

The Norden bombsight was so classified and considered so important that army air corps personnel who were to be trained to use it had to take an oath of secrecy before even seeing one. The somber oath follows in its entirety:

> *Mindful of the secret trust about to be placed in me by my commander-in-chief, the president of the United States, by whose direction I have been chosen for bombardier training, and mindful of the fact that I am to become guardian of one of my country's most priceless military assets, the American bombsight, I do here, in the presence of Almighty God, swear by the bombardier's code of honor to keep inviolate the secrecy of any and all confidential information revealed to me, and further to uphold the honor and integrity of the army air forces, if need be, with my life itself.*

Because of the secret work being conducted at the company and at Carl Norden's Manhattan facility, security was especially tight. Photographs show the plants surrounded by barbed wire. Each plant was guarded by highly trained and armed guards.

Incredibly, a member of the German spy network was still able to steal the blueprints for the bombsight. Hermann Lang, a naturalized German immigrant, was able to get a job in Norden's plant. He worked late into the night, copying the blueprints, and was able to get the copies on board a ship bound for Germany. He later made his way to Germany, where he was paid $3,000 by the Third Reich and was toasted as a hero by the Luftwaffe's chief, Herman Goering. Ironically, except for the $3,000 paid to him by the Luftwaffe, his efforts were for nothing. The Germans never incorporated the bombsight, one of America's top secrets, on their planes.

Betrayed by a double agent, Lang was arrested by the FBI as one of the "Nazi 19" group of spies. He went to trial in Brooklyn, New York, in what was the largest trial of spies in U.S. history. The group received a combined sentence of over three hundred years in jail. Lang was sentenced to eighteen years in a federal prison.

Intent on sabotaging American industrial plants, on the day Germany declared war on America, December 11, 1941, Hitler authorized funding to train saboteurs. Eight saboteurs were placed by two submarines on shore in New York and Florida with a prioritized list of plants the füehrer wanted destroyed or damaged.

On June 12, 1942, *U-202* pulled within fifty feet of the beach near Amagansett, New York. George Dasch, Ernst Burger, Richard Quirin and Heinrich Heinck were rowed ashore on rubber rafts. Four nights later, on June 16, 1942, *U-584* sneaked close to the shore south of Jacksonville, Florida, at Ponte Vedra Beach. Edward John Kerling, Hermann Otto Neubauer, Werner Thiel and Herbert Haupt swam ashore.

Plants such as the Carl Norden plant in Manhattan, New York, were on the list that the FBI found in the pocket of one of the spies when he was arrested. The headline of the *New York Times* announced the capture of all Eight Nazi spies as follows:

FBI Seizes 8 Saboteurs Landed by U-Boats Here and in Florida to Blow up War Plants, Invaders Confess Had TNT to Blast Key Factories

The trial for the eight that was held in Washington, D.C., concluded on August 1, 1942. For turning in the others, Dasch received a sentence of thirty years in prison, and Burger received a life sentence. The other six went to the electric chair on August 8, 1942. Six years later, the sentences of the two whose lives had been spared were commuted, and they were relocated to the American Zone of occupied Germany. Their countrymen treated them as traitors because it was felt that they had caused the deaths of their comrades. Both died without ever receiving the pardons that they said had been promised to them by FBI director J. Edgar Hoover for cooperating with the government.

Each of the saboteurs was allowed to write a letter home. Edward Kerling, committed to Nazism to the very end, wrote to his wife:

> *Marie, my wife—I am with you to the last minute! This will help me to take it as a German! Even the heaven out there is dark. It's raining. Our graves are far from home, but not forgotten. Marie, until we meet in a better world! May God be with you. My love to you, my heart to my country.*
> *Heil Hitler!*
> *Your Ed, always*

For America, the use of Norden bombsights did not end with the close of World War II. During the Korean conflict, B-29s, with their aging bombsights, were used extensively. Then in Vietnam, they were once again pressed into service. By this time, the air force had to recall some of the World War II technicians in order to make the bombsights operational again. The bombsight's final mission occurred in 1967 with Naval Air Operations Squadron Sixty-Seven in Operation Igloo White to help with the placement of air-delivered seismic detectors along the Ho Chi Minh Trail.

While Carl Norden furnished most of the bombsights for America during the war, he was not the only inventor developing and manufacturing bombsights for the U.S. military. In the 1930s, the Sperry Corporation developed and tested its version of a bombsight. Even though officials in the War Department did not regard it as highly as Norden's, they reluctantly gave approval for it, as Norden was having difficulty meeting the government's large demands for the device. Sperry went a little further than Norden by furnishing, combined in a complete assembly, its version of the bombsight with its already established autopilot. The army air corps purchased 5,563 of these units that it used exclusively on its B-24 Liberator bombers. The company furnished bellows assemblies for all of Sperry's bombsights.

10

WAR COMES TO AMERICA

For several years prior to the beginning of World War II, members of the U.S. government's military readiness panel had continued their visits to the company. The panel knew of the company's capabilities and had a plan in place for it in case of war. At that time, there were about five hundred employees working for the company.

The thoughtful planning soon paid dividends, as a war followed Japan's attack on the U.S. fleet at Pearl Harbor that killed almost three thousand sailors and airmen. Most Americans were listening to their radios when President Franklin Roosevelt declared, "Yesterday, December 7, 1941, a date that will live in infamy, the United States of America was suddenly and deliberately attacked by naval and air forces of the empire of Japan." The United States declared war on Japan, and then Germany declared war on the United States.

In a time of serious speeches from world leaders, Great Britain's Winston Churchill said, "You ask: what is our aim? I can answer in one word: victory. Victory at all costs. Victory in spite of all terror. Victory however long and hard the road may be. For without victory, there is no survival." President Roosevelt added, "No man can tame a tiger by stroking it. There can be no appeasement with ruthlessness. There can be no reasoning with an incendiary bomb. We know now that a nation can have peace with the Nazis only at the price of total surrender."

At that time, Americans knew that the horrors of war had come to them. They had no way, however, of knowing that approximately 16 million of their men and women would be joining the fight, nor did they know that about 396,000 would never return home.

After the attack on Pearl Harbor, Japan's Admiral Yamamoto, a Harvard University graduate, said prophetically that Japan and its allies would lose the war because the sleeping giant that was American industry had been awakened. One of those "sleeping giants," the company, was located at 2318 Kingston Pike in Knoxville, Tennessee. It awakened quickly, because it and the military readiness panel had done their homework. It required only the procurement of some heavier press equipment and the addition of some buildings within the plant area.

The company was ready within weeks. Employment there eventually reached four thousand. Working three shifts, seven days a week, with many workers doing double shifts of sixteen hours, the materiel that workers at the company produced can best be described as incredible. The full extent of the Fulton Company's contributions to the nation's wartime needs have never been published prior to this work.

WAR BONDS

Americans were asked to buy government-issued war bonds (loans to the government) as a way of financing the very expensive war that had just begun. The average annual income for workers at that time was about $2,000, and the population was being asked to buy bonds regularly.

Bonds were bought at 75 percent of their face value in denominations between $25 and $10,000, and they reached maturity in ten years. This meant that even though they were called "the greatest investment on earth," the buyers were paid back at a paltry annual rate of 2.9 percent. The War Finance Committee and the War Advertising Council conducted the largest advertising campaign the country had ever seen to sell bonds. To help finance the advertising campaign, companies and private citizens donated more than $250 million.

All-hands rallies were regularly scheduled by the company as it attempted to encourage its employees to buy war bonds. This, of course, helped finance the war—the same war that it was working so hard to help win. Movie stars and other well-known entertainers routinely toured the country, promoting the sale of war bonds. The "Stars Over America" bond tour, in which 337 stars participated, sold over $838 million in war bonds. Most movies made during the war years showed the war bond logo when the credits rolled at the end. These war bond logos can still be seen today at the end of classic movies from that era. Not to be outdone, professional baseball arranged a special kind of game among the three New York–area teams: the New York Yankees, New York Giants and Brooklyn Dodgers. A ticket for this unusual game went toward the purchase of a war bond. Each of the teams was allowed six times at bat. No one paid much attention to the final score, which was Dodgers, 5; Yankees, 1; and Giants, 0. The United States government was the big winner of the game, taking in $56,500,000 in "ticket" sales.

One of the company's rallies featured Kate Smith, a popular singer at the time, who delighted the crowd of employees when she sang her iconic hit song "God Bless America." Because of the threat caused by Adolf Hitler and the Nazis in Germany, Irving Berlin, in 1938, rewrote his 1918 song in the form of a prayer and gave the rights for it to Smith.

A thunderous ovation began as Smith's powerful voice belted out the last lines of the famous tune to her audience of awestruck factory workers:

> *God bless America,*
> *Land that I love.*
> *Stand beside her*
> *And guide her*
> *Through the night*
> *With a light from above.*
>
> *From the mountains*
> *To the prairies*
> *To the oceans*
> *White with foam.*
> *God bless America,*
> *My home sweet home.*

By the end of the war, 85 million Americans, more than half of the population, had bought war bonds. Due to the government's massive efforts, it received from the sale of bonds a total of $185.7 billion.

THE PAYOFF

Helping fulfill the prophecy of Admiral Yamamoto, American industry, the sleeping giant, rolled up its sleeves and went to work to win a war.

Many of those sleeves belonged to inexperienced women who were willing to learn on the job and quickly enter the workforce. Men who were considered too old to fight by the military also made up a large portion of the workforce. By the end of the war, 8 million women were working in defense plants. Norman Rockwell's Rosie the Riveter, with her sleeves rolled up, showing her muscles, and the resolve on her face, represented this army of women workers. This blend of women and older men would be so successful that it stunned the navy liaison officers who maintained offices at the company.

The ninety-six thousand B-17, B-24, B-25, B-26 and B-29 bombers built during the war had over one hundred of Fulton's bellows assemblies in their air frames and instruments, along with six on their bombsights. The following table is a partial list of the company's immense and important contributions to the army, navy and army air corps between 1942 and 1945.

Bellows for various uses	53,000,000
Hand grenade fuses	50,000,000
Shell boosters	44,000,000
Bellows assemblies for aircraft instruments	25,000,000
Other bellows assemblies	11,000,000
Five-inch-diameter shell casings	11,000,000
Tail-fin assemblies for 60-mm and 81-mm mortar shells	8,000,000
Thermostats	3,000,000
Bellows for use in various instruments	2,500,000
20mm steel shells	1,500,000
40mm steel shells	500,000
37mm steel shells	150,000
Bomb fuses	325,000
100-pound practice bombs	300,000
Aneroid assemblies for oxygen regulators	250,000
Ventilation regulators for navy and maritime ships	180,000
1.1-inch magazines for cartridges	150,000
Barrel reflectors for machine guns	150,000
Bellows for 20,000 Norden bombsights	120,000
Tail-fin assemblies for demolition bombs	100,000
Regulators for war production processes	100,000
Detonator fuse bases	70,000
Manifold pressure indicator for aircraft engines	50,000
Valves for navy and coast guard ships	40,000

Diesel controls for navy ships	30,000
Cowl flap actuators for aircraft	20,000
Air position indicators for carrier-based planes	2,000
Bellows-seal valves for the Manhattan Project (estimated)	5,000
Bellows assemblies for use on atomic bombs	2

B-29 SUPERFORTRESS

Built by Boeing Aircraft Company, the B-29 Superfortress had dozens of bellows manufactured by the company in various onboard applications. These included one in each of the plane's two altimeters; six on its Norden bombsight; more than one hundred in its airframe, serving as flexible connectors; and, finally, one on the atomic bomb it carried.

Four thousand of the bombers were built in the early 1940s. Boeing's first test flight of the aircraft occurred on September 21, 1942. The demand for the large bombers was so great, especially in the Pacific theater of the war, that they often went into action while thousands of engineering changes were still being made.

The B-29 was 99 feet long and had a wingspan of 141 feet. It weighed 105,000 pounds and had a top speed of 365 miles per hour. With a crew of ten, it had a ceiling of 32,000 feet and a range of 5,800 miles. The airplane's armament consisted of twelve .50-caliber machine guns, one 20-millimeter cannon and a bombload capacity of 20,000 pounds.

Technologically advanced for the time, the B-29 had guns that could be fired by remote control. Two crew areas, fore and aft, were pressurized, and crew members could crawl between the two areas. The tail gunners' compartment was pressurized but could not be reached from the other areas.

AIRCRAFT ALTIMETERS

Fulton's bellows were already invented, patented and in full production by the time airplanes were developed. Using the bellows as a barometer to measure barometric pressure and its changes was one of the earliest uses of them. With the advent of the airplane, a means to constantly monitor the aircrafts' altitude was of paramount importance. Designers and builders of airplanes immediately adopted the barometer as their instrument of choice and called it an altimeter.

The pressure barometer, also known as an aneroid barometer, measures atmospheric pressure, or the weight of the atmosphere above the instrument. It operates on the principle that atmospheric pressure increases or decreases with changes in altitude. The altimeter is placed inside a case that is connected by a tube to a static port outside the airplane. Inside the case is a bellows from which air has been evacuated. Using gears, pinions, springs and a shaft, the contraction or expansion of the bellows causes the movement of a pointer on a dial that resembles a clock. In this case, the big hand indicates hundreds of feet of altitude, and the little hand indicates thousands of feet of altitude. Because atmospheric pressure is measured relative to sea level, a pressure altimeter is adjusted by turning a knob to compensate for small changes in barometric pressure caused by location changes of the aircraft.

An improved version of the pressure-type altimeter was developed by an inventor named Paul Kollsman, who patented it in 1936. His version of the altimeter is still in use.

SPLITTING ATOMS

Around 400 BCE, the Greek Philosopher Democritus stated that all things on earth were made up of "atoms" that were indestructible, indivisible and in constant motion. In 1905, Albert Einstein introduced his theory of relativity. His simple sounding yet profound formula of $e=mc^2$ (energy equals mass times the speed of light squared) would lead to him being called the father of physics. After reviewing Einstein's work, scientists, especially those in Germany and America, were becoming convinced that splitting Democritus's atom was within the realm of possibility.

Scientists in the late 1930s, realizing that the splitting of the atom was becoming likely, knew that a tremendous amount of energy would be unlocked with it. With this in mind, American scientists, several of whom had recently emigrated from Germany, convinced President Franklin Roosevelt that their German counterparts were working toward developing a nuclear bomb.

In 1939, one of the scientists, Leo Szilard, an emigrant from Hungary, thought it was very important for the president of the United States to know that a weapon that would alter a war could soon be built and that the Germans were getting close to developing such a weapon. He wrote the first of four letters to the president on August 2, 1939. Knowing that the president would not know him and would likely ignore letters signed by him, Szilard asked his well-known close friend Albert Einstein to sign his letters to the president. His first letter follows in its entirety:

> *F.D. Roosevelt*
> *President of the United States*
> *White House*
> *Washington, D.C.*
>
> *Sir:*
> *Some recent work by E. Fermi and L. Szilard, which has been communicated to me in manuscript, leads me to expect that the element uranium may be turned into a new and important source of energy in the immediate future.*
> *In the course of the last four months, it has been made probable, through the work of Joliot in France as well as Fermi and Szilard in America, that it may become possible to set up a nuclear chain reaction in a large mass of uranium, by which vast amounts of power and large quantities of new radium-like elements would be generated. A single bomb of this type, carried by boat and exploded in a port, might very well destroy the whole port, together with some of the surrounding territory.*
>
> *Albert Einstein*

Incredibly, the subterfuge of Szilard's letters signed by Einstein convinced President Roosevelt that action was required. Based on the information from the scientists, President Roosevelt immediately initiated the secret Manhattan Project that would lead to America's development of the atomic bomb.

HELPING BRING AN END TO A BRUTAL WAR

The B-29 heavy bomber and the P-51 fighter plane arrived just in time. The nuclear bombs the bombers would need to carry weighed about ten thousand pounds each, and the B-29s provided the platform needed to fly great distances. The P-51s were capable of providing escort for the large planes on most missions.

By the evening of August 5, 1945, the uranium version of the atomic bomb, "Little Boy," was fully assembled and ready for arming once the B-29 took off and was at altitude. Around midnight, the bomb was hydraulically hoisted into the bomb bay of the bomber *Enola Gay*. Most of the in-the-know group of scientists and military personnel felt that the bomb would alter the course of the war and, in doing so, change the world. President Harry Truman, some members of Congress and top military leaders knew of the planned action and waited nervously for news.

To help minimize the risk of Little Boy prematurely exploding, a multistage arming system was designed. A pin was manually inserted and kept in place until just before the bomb was dropped. When the bomb left the B-29, a timer powered by a twenty-four-volt battery prevented detonation for a minimum of fifteen seconds to ensure the safety of the aircraft. At that point, a barometric pressure switch incorporating a Fulton Company bellows activated the system at an altitude of 6,600 feet. Finally, altitude-sensing radar, using a version of the Japanese-developed Yagi antenna, triggered the detonation of the bomb at the desired altitude of 1,890 feet.

At 2:45 a.m. on August 6, the bomber's four two-thousand horsepower Wright Cyclone engines roared to life. Colonel Paul Tibbets said on his radio, "Dimples eight two to North Tinian tower. We are ready for take-off on runway Able." Six other B-29s and several P-51 fighter planes flew escort.

About six miles above the Japanese city of Hiroshima, the *Enola Gay* lunged upward when the ten-thousand-pound payload fell from the airplane's bomb bay. Three days later, Captain Chuck Sweeney, flying another B-29 named *Bock's Car*, dropped a plutonium-powered bomb on the city of Nagasaki. Six days later, on August 15, 1945, the emperor of Japan agreed to the surrender terms that America and its allies had laid out three weeks earlier.

As the giant B-29s flew to and from their destinations, the fingerprints of East Tennesseans were abundant. The wings, fuselages and vertical and horizontal stabilizers were clad in aluminum made by Alcoa's Aluminum Company of America. The pilots and gunners peered through Plexiglas that was made by Knoxville's Rohm and Haas Chemical Company. From the company came the more than one hundred bellows in the plane's airframe. The company also furnished one bellows for each of its two altimeters, six bellows on its Norden bombsight and one bellows on each atomic bomb as part of the detonation system. The uranium-235 that powered the first atomic bomb was enriched in Oak Ridge, Tennessee.

ARMY-NAVY "E" AWARD

During World War II, the Army-Navy "E" award was given to industrial facilities that reached and maintained excellence in the manufacturing of war materiel. The award was intended to give some of the government's most important suppliers encouragement to produce as much as possible. All factories were eligible to receive the award.

Manufacturers were nominated for the award by the chiefs of the government supply agencies, district procurement officers and the commanding officers of the materiel commands. The evaluated categories were:

- Quality and quantity of production.
- Overcoming of production obstacles.
- Avoidance of work stoppages.
- Maintaining fair labor standards.
- Training of additional labor forces.
- Good record keeping in relation to health and safety.

The award consisted of a pennant for the company and small individual pins for all employees. The pennant was a triangular swallowtail banner with a white border and a capital "E" within a yellow wreath of oak and laurel leaves on a blue-and-red background. Plants that maintained an outstanding record for six months after receiving their initial "E" award were given a white star to be placed on their pennant. If the companies kept their outstanding performance, they received an additional star.

Generally, a naval officer and an army officer would attend a ceremony when the award was presented. After the award was given to the company, employees would receive their individual pins.

A company magazine advertisement during the war reflected the earned pride of its employees, who were doing their jobs in the defense of their country. An Army-Navy "E" was shown with a caption that read as follows: "Proudly, we fly the coveted Army-Navy 'E' flag with added star, signifying continued compliance with requirements for over six months, presented to the Fulton Sylphon Company for high achievement in the production of war materials."

During the war, 4,283 companies were granted the award. This represented about 5 percent of the eligible defense-related factories. By the end of the war, the company had received its fifth white star—the most possible in the industrial category.

Opposite, top: "E" Award ceremony in front of a barbed-wire gate. *Courtesy of Jerry Riggs.*

Opposite, bottom: Proud employees holding their "E" Award banner. *Courtesy of Jerry Riggs.*

This page, top: Assembly department employees. *Author's collection.*

This page, bottom: Weston Fulton and Admiral Wat Cluverius at an "E" Award ceremony. *Courtesy of Jerry Riggs.*

Above: Employees at an "E" Award ceremony. *Courtesy of Jerry Riggs.*

Left: Original "E" Award plaque in the present-day company lobby. *Author's collection.*

The Army-Navy "E" Award, normally given only to industries, was granted to Iowa State College (now Iowa State University) for its contribution to the production of uranium for the Manhattan Project. The school developed the Ames Process for the extraction, purification and mass production of uranium. The award program was terminated three months after the war ended.

THE NAVY'S FIVE-INCH .38-CALIBER GUN

Used on battleships, cruisers and destroyers, the Mark 12 five-inch gun was used by the U.S. Navy between 1934 and 2008 and was generally

Above: Five-inch guns on USS *North Carolina*. *Author's collection.*

Right: Five-inch shell casings. *Author's collection.*

recognized as the navy's most versatile weapon. It could be used against surface and aircraft targets. The gun fired a projectile that was five inches in diameter and weighed fifty-five pounds. The bore of the chrome-plated barrel had right-hand twist rifling. The average life of a barrel was about 4,600 firings.

Firing at a forty-five-degree angle, the projectile could be hurled eighteen thousand yards, or more than ten miles. When used as an antiaircraft weapon, it could fire a projectile up to thirty-seven thousand feet. A fully trained crew could fire as many as twenty-two rounds per minute. On average, one-thousand rounds had to be fired to bring down an enemy airplane, which was generally brought down by fragments of the exploding shell, not direct hits.

During the war, the U.S. Navy fired over 22 million of the five-inch .38-caliber shells. The company supplied one-half, or 11 million of these shells. Until the 1970s, navy maintenance crews came to the company to service and keep in good working condition the machinery that had been used to make the five-inch shells.

THE BRITISH CONNECTION

The achievements of the company during the war years, 1942 to 1945, appropriately enough, brought to mind Winston Churchill's famous quote, "Never in the field of human conflict was so much owed by so many to so few." After the war, it was learned that the company had also been secretly helping the United States' British ally.

A few months after the end of the war, it was announced that the company had furnished more than half of the bellows that Great Britain had used for its bombsights. The British referred to the seven bellows assemblies on their version of the bombsights as computers.

The English bombsights were mainly used on bombers that went on nighttime raids or those that took part in pattern bombing missions. While it did not quite offer the accuracy of the American bombsight, Britain's military leaders thought it offered them enough strategic advantages to consider its production vital to their country's national defense. Representatives of the British military, always traveling in nondescript traditional business suits, often came to visit the company in Knoxville to confer on engineering issues and check the progress of orders for bellows assemblies. Because of their distinctive British accents, in an attempt to maintain complete secrecy, when traveling in this country, they would avoid speaking any more than was absolutely necessary. Consequently, very few people, including those who worked at the company, knew of the secret arrangement that continued until the war's end.

TIME FOR CELEBRATION

During the war, a close working relationship was maintained between the company and W.J. Savage Company, which was owned by Weston Fulton. Because of this close connection, many parts for the several secret projects the company worked on were furnished by the Savage Company. Fulton was personally honored in early 1945 by President Roosevelt when he was given a Certificate of Appreciation for his efforts and for the many contributions his inventions made during the war. A popular saying at the time was, "Fulton's bellows are an essential part of everything that rolls, floats, shoots or flies."

After forty-five agonizingly long months, the war, for America, had come to an end. Its 16 million soldiers, sailors and airmen were coming home to a jubilant country that had danced in the streets with the announcement from the Japanese emperor that his country had surrendered. All agreed it was time for celebration.

After working long, bone-wearying shifts and living under the strain of news from the various war fronts, company employees, along with the rest of the country, celebrated the end of the war. Management at the company and navy personnel put on a memorable show a few days after the company had received its fifth and final white star for its "E" banner.

Now that secrecy was no longer a concern, the company gave the employees permission to invite members of their family to the plant for a day of celebration. The employees and their family members were able to walk through displays, such as a blue navy fighter plane, a tank, a jeep, a truck and a navy boat—all incorporating Fulton's invention, the seamless metal flexible bellows, that had been manufactured by the company in vast numbers. Coincidentally, the spectacular display was set up beside the department where the 11 million five-inch shells had been made for the navy. At seven years of age, the author of this book accompanied his grandfather Walter Weaver, who worked in the company's bellows assembly department, to the memorable celebration and currently has his grandfather's "E" Medal lapel pin.

Even though the company, in conjunction with the navy, put on an impressive celebration party, it could not match that of Manhattan's Carl L. Norden Company. That company, which had just received its third star for its "E" pennant, hired the Ringling Brothers to entertain its employees and clients in Madison Square Garden.

Americans suddenly had more free time. They could go to the movies and ball games, and now, there was even enough gasoline to enable them to take drives around the countryside. The management at the company, recognizing the importance of recreation and relaxation for its employees, encouraged and sponsored teams in several sports, including softball, baseball and basketball.

Just outside the assembly department, a horseshoe pit was installed. Every day during the morning and afternoon break times, the pitchers would throw the shoes, while the remainder of the employees watched. The pitchers got so good that they were disappointed if they did not throw a strike on just about every pitch.

The baseball team, comprised exclusively of employees, was especially good. An ultimate compliment was given to this team by former Cincinnati Reds catcher Ed Bailey. The National League all-star veteran once told the writer of this book, "This might surprise you, but one of the best teams I ever played against was that of the Fulton Company in Knoxville, Tennessee. They were hard to beat. I can still remember several of the player's names—Ralph White, Henry Brown, Hubert Davenport, Clarence Palmer."

Like during World War I, several medical advances were made during World War II. Two of these are still very much in use today. Learning that blood could be stored on ice for up to a month, blood banks were established to be used for necessary transfusions. Plastic surgery also came about at this time to reconstruct the faces of those who had been badly injured.

11

UNFULFILLED PLANS

In the years immediately following World War II, the economy was booming, houses were being built in unprecedented numbers and millions of babies were becoming the baby boomer generation. For almost everyone, the outlook was brighter and, in some ways, similar to the beginning of the twentieth century. In 1946, in this kind of beginning-again atmosphere, Weston Fulton made a big announcement as he approached seventy-five years of age.

The *Knoxville News-Sentinel* reported in its Sunday Magazine section headline, "Weston M. Fulton, Father of Sylphon, is Planning New Postwar Enterprise Here." Further, it reported that after Fulton had sold his company, he had not been just sitting back, watching while his "little sylphon invention went to war on land, sea, and air in hundreds of vital capacities. The inventor, financier, and one-time weatherman has been lugging right along in his research laboratory." The laboratory was located in his W.J. Savage Company.

Fulton had decided to build a new $250,000 plant to manufacture the brainchild that he had been working on during the past few years. He was developing a non-clogging furnace stoker. He said it would be automatic and compared it to an electric refrigerator. He went on, "In fact, it'll suit us if our future stoker users will simply start a furnace fire in the fall, then lock up their furnace room and stay out until spring."

The stoker would automatically dispose of all ashes and clinkers down to a minute residue. While doing this and generating heat, it would be entirely smokeless. Additionally, it would feed on the cheapest type of coal, which was about one-half the price of regular stoker coal.

Fulton purchased sixteen acres of land in Knoxville's Sharp's Gap area next to the Southern Railway tracks. Some of the equipment that was to be used would come from Fulton's W.J. Savage Company. The building would only have one floor to ease the handling of heavy material. His initial plans were to hire about one hundred employees and expand production steadily after that. He indicated that he expected his son Robert would eventually run the business and added, "Meanwhile, I'll be around, looking after things."

Fulton reported that the stoker was well past the laboratory stage and ready to be mass produced as soon as the new plant was ready. He said that he planned to test several of the units in representative Knoxville homes in the coming winter.

Sadly, for the inventor, winter never came. On the morning of May 16, 1946, Weston Fulton and his fertile mind passed away. His shocked family said he had died suddenly and unexpectedly. His latest plans would never be implemented. The project Fulton had so much confidence in died with him.

It was front-page news in many newspapers. The *Knoxville Journal* reported:

> *Weston Miller Fulton Knoxville inventor, scientist, and manufacturer, whose inventile genius led to the development of the "sylphon device" for thermostatic control of temperatures, died suddenly of a heart seizure at 9:30 a.m. yesterday at his home on Lyons View Pike. Mr. Fulton collapsed while shaving and died in a few minutes. He had apparently been enjoying his usual health and had been normally active for the past few days.*

On the evening of Fulton's death, the *Knoxville News-Sentinel*'s headline read, "Weston Fulton, Knox Inventor Dies at Home." A front-page article indicated, "His family members reported that Mr. Fulton had given no previous indication of ill health and went on to say that Mr. Fulton was a friendly fellow. Jovial and hearty, he was quick with repartee and joking remarks." The article reported that mere acquaintances of his said, "That man always gives me a lift, just the way he speaks." One of Fulton's close friends said, "He knew more things about everything than any man I've ever seen in my life." The article went on, "One of the wealthiest men in the state, business associates tell that he 'just had a knack for making a business succeed.' Always open-handed, he gave generously to many charities and helped many persons, both close associates and those remote."

Because of Fulton's notoriety, newspapers in several countries carried the news of his death. An example of this is the English version of an excerpt from a Portuguese newspaper's obituary that read, "He produced numerous improvements in scientific instruments employed by the Weather Observatory, which were soon adopted by the government. These improvements and their descriptions were published in the pamphlet *The Fulton Automatic River Gage*....Included among his inventions were the depth charge and the thermostat."

Weston Miller Fulton's funeral was held at 3:30 p.m. on Saturday, May 18, in Mann's Mortuary in Knoxville. Reverend E.B. McGukin officiated. Fulton's pallbearers included University of Tennessee president J.D. Hoskins, company general manager C.N. Mynderse and two future company general managers, Jean Giesler and Freeman Cross. He was laid to rest in the family plot in front of the columns of their Greek-style monument in Highland Memorial Cemetery, located just off Knoxville's Sutherland Avenue.

Most of Fulton's grandchildren were too young to remember much about their grandfather; some were not even born when he passed away. They learned from their parents about the generous and caring man they never knew. Jay Talley III, his sister Kathy Todd and Jeff Hartley speak of their grandfather with great respect. The same is true for his nieces Ruth Tiedemann and Martha Fulton Wells.

Ruth "Sunnye" Tiedemann told of the time when her family was visiting the Fultons at the Westcliff mansion during World War II, and she asked a question about the location of Germany. As a seven-year-old, she was impressed that her famous uncle took her question seriously and spent time showing her the location of Germany.

It was obvious that Fulton never forgot his roots. In the early 1900s, when his business had become successful, he financed the purchase of a large farm in Alabama for two of his brothers. He provided them with all of the required farm equipment and stocked the farm with a herd of dairy cows.

Fulton enjoyed a friendly game of cards and going to the movies, and he was well known as one of the city's most gracious hosts at Westcliff. Interestingly, during World War II, no parties of any sort were held at the mansion. In addition to their trips to Europe, in the 1940s, Fulton took his family, by train, to the Rose Bowl when the University of Tennessee played the University of Southern California. Picture after picture show the closeness of the family. The way Fulton felt about his family was illustrated by the unique playhouse he had constructed for his children.

Their little house had hot and cold running water and a fully functioning kitchen and bathroom.

Two years after Fulton's death, five clean-energy-type patents were issued that pertained to his work on the automatic stoker project. The patent office assigned them to the inventor's wife, Barbara, and their son Robert. However, the patents were, by that time, largely meaningless. Just how big an effect his idea of an automatic smokeless furnace would have had in the 1940s can only be imagined.

12

THE SCHOOL THEY NAMED FOR HIM

In 1948, the Knoxville, Tennessee School Board authorized the construction of four new high schools. The new schools, located in the city's quadrants, would be called South High, West High, East High, and Fulton High (not North High as would have been expected). The reputation of Weston Fulton as a hands-on industrialist and early advocate for vocational training was obviously on the minds of the school board members with this unexpected decision.

From its inception, Fulton High School (officially Weston M. Fulton High School) has had a dual curriculum—both academic and vocational. The naming of Thomas H. Johnston from nearby Stair Technical School as the school's first principal further indicates the school board's total commitment to the technical vocational curriculum.

On March 5, 1949, a groundbreaking ceremony, initiating construction of the new school, was held. The school opened in September 1951. Vocational training was offered in the following fields: sheet metal, drafting, cosmetology, radio, machining, commercial art, printing, auto mechanics, photography, electrical working, cooking, woodworking, television and refrigeration. This educational approach for a high school was revolutionary, and Fulton High was one of the first in the South to offer such a curriculum.

Additionally, some students, especially veterans, were allowed to take some of the vocational courses without being required to take the "core" classes, such as English and mathematics. Several Quonset hut buildings were constructed near the main school building for these students.

Above: Fulton High School
entrance. *Author's collection.*

Right: Seth Smith, Fulton
High School principal.
Author's collection.

Entrance to the School of Communications. *Author's collection.*

Russell Mayes, director of the School of Communications. *Author's collection.*

Mascot sign in school hall. *Author's collection.*

The new school adopted a mascot of a falcon because falcons are "strong fliers that soar high into the sky." The school newspaper was the *Falcon Quill,* and the yearbook was simply named *The Falcon.* The school's motto became: "Enter to learn; go forth to serve."

Since the opening of the school, radio classes have been very popular. Very few high schools across the nation have their own student-operated radio station. In the state of Tennessee, there are only four such schools. Fulton's station, WKCS, was first on the air on December 18, 1952.

Russell Mayes is the current leader in the field of communications, which includes radio classes. Under his leadership, the Fulton High School Communications Department has become a magnet school for that curriculum. This means that anyone in the county who desires to major in communications can now transfer to Fulton High School to pursue a career in that field.

ATHLETICS

Ever since the school's opening, its programs in several sports have been among the best in the greater Knoxville area. Every year, a significant number of college scouts visit in an effort to recruit Fulton High athletes coached by long-time football coach Rob Black and popular basketball coach Jody Wright.

The many outstanding athletes the school has produced include the following: Robert Rovere, a track star who became a six-time all-American at East Tennessee State University; Jackie Walker, a linebacker at the University of Tennessee; D.D. Lewis, a linebacker for Mississippi State University and the Dallas Cowboys; Ron Widby, a star in four sports and punter for the University of Tennessee and teams in the National Football League; and Jay Bayless, a three-sport star and basketball player at the University of Kentucky.

THE WINDS OF CHANGE

In the last several years, Fulton High School has undergone several changes. In the early 1990s, the school narrowly escaped being closed and merged with another school, Austin-East High. The plan that was discussed by the school board called for a new school to be built that would combine the two schools. After long discussions, members of the school board finally decided that a better answer would be to leave the two schools intact and spend the money that would have been spent on the new school to upgrade and modernize the two schools. This idea carried the day, and most now agree that it was a sound decision.

Still, a dismal graduation rate reflected the poor morale of Fulton High School students and teachers alike. A study in 2006 showed that fewer than 7 percent of Fulton graduates had graduated from college after six years. Another study showed that academic achievement rates were decreasing among the current students. The faculty was wondering if the school was living up to its own motto: "Enter to learn, go forth to serve."

Fulton High School supporters, by the hundreds, played an active and vocal role in discouraging the proposed change. Subpar performance continued for a few more years, until the newly appointed principal, Dr. Jon Rysewyk, decided to make some dramatic changes.

When Dr. Rysewyk discussed the dire situation with the teachers and told them some of the changes he had in mind, forty-six of them decided they were not up to what was to be asked of them. Several thought the situation was hopeless, and others felt they were not physically able to do what was going to be expected of them. Replacement teachers signed an agreement to work twenty-one extra school days while receiving a signing bonus of $3,000.

THE SCHOOL'S DRAMATIC TURNAROUND

Today, when entering the halls of the school, one senses an atmosphere of success. The confident, friendly smiles of the students indicate that something out of the ordinary is happening. Students, teachers and the administration are noticeably proud of the journey that they and those before them have been on. The drudgery often associated with going to school has largely been replaced with an air of, "See? We told you we could do it."

The ingredients of this success, while seemingly simple, were very effective. Starting in 2007, the school was divided into five homogenous groups. The groups, which wear different color shirts to denote each, are as follows: ninth grade (maroon), tenth grade (blue), School of Health Sciences (white) and School of Skilled Professions, (gray). Each student stays with the same core group of teachers for a two-year period, allowing the students in each particular group to get to know each other and their teachers better.

It was only after much discussion and hand wringing that the dress code was adopted. With very little complaint, the dress code has been successful and now seems to offer a sense of pride for each group. The students see this as being part of a "team." Some of the eighth graders, when preparing to enter Fulton High School, know about the program and ask when they will be able to get their uniform. No one expected this.

In order to give each student as much individual attention as possible, each group has its own principal, guidance counselor and student advocate. Therefore, the school has five principals and an executive principal. The importance of an easily approachable guidance counselor was shown in Fulton High School alumnus Earl Well's college master's thesis from 1964. In his work, identifying a career path early on that a student is comfortable with and has an interest in was shown to dramatically increase the student's chances of future success.

The current principal, Seth Smith, said, "We continue to try to provide an education for our students that will give them the best possible opportunity in whatever field they choose to enter." Further, Smith explained a somewhat unexpected opportunity that potentially emerged when the City of Knoxville moved its police department and fire department into the nearby building that was formerly St. Mary's Hospital. With the envisioned cooperation of the city, the proximity will allow students who are interested in law enforcement or firefighting to learn firsthand through on-the-job training. Smith said the decision to offer criminal justice as a major has already been made.

Left: Rebecca Henry, English language learning teacher. *Author's collection.*

Right: Names of some star students. *Author's collection.*

The University of Tennessee offers four-year "flagship scholarships" to qualifying students at thirty-eight flagship high schools in Tennessee. Fulton High School is one of these designated schools, and Smith indicated that Fulton students are strongly encouraged to take advantage of this unique and valuable opportunity.

With an agreement between the State of Tennessee and Ford Motor Company, Ford offers three vocational training programs, and Fulton High School participates in all of them. The Automotive Student Service Educational Training Program allows students to earn while they learn. Students alternate about every eight weeks between their classroom and a sponsoring Ford dealership. After two years, the students have earned an associate degree in addition to valuable dealership experience.

Ford's Accelerated Credential Training Program calls for fifteen weeks of specialized Ford training. Because Ford partners with the Universal Technical Institute for training, employment opportunities are available nationwide.

The third vocational training program offered by Ford is Maintenance and Light Repair. The students learn the core skills needed for a career with Ford.

Left: Book of Weston Fulton's patents in school lobby. *Author's collection.*

Below: Monthly meeting of former Fulton High School students. *Courtesy of Dana Howard.*

For several years, the Emerald Youth Foundation has contributed to the success of the school. The foundation provides companionship for the students who it hopes will eventually become role models in their respective communities. Students come to the foundation year-round for sports, games and other activities. During the school year, the students whose parents have consented are picked up from school and taken to the foundation's headquarters, where qualified, professional teachers help them with their lessons in the subjects they have difficulties with. About 25 percent of the students at the foundation attend Fulton High School.

Through the hard work of the last three executive principals in particular—Dr. Jon Rysewyk, Rob Speas and Seth Smith—the school that was named for Weston Fulton continues to flourish. The school's motto, "Enter to learn, go forth to serve," seems to fit very well.

Throughout the years, Weston Fulton's oil portrait—the one that was presented to the school by his family in 1951—is still on display in the school's lobby. Just under the portrait, in a glass case, is a book that contains many of Fulton's original engineering drawings and descriptions of his patents.

13

MODERN-DAY ENGINEERS CONTINUE TO FIND NEW APPLICATIONS FOR FULTON'S INVENTIONS

Even though Fulton sold his company in 1930 and passed away in 1946, his bellows are still popular with design engineers who have problems that need to be solved related to temperature and pressure. With his patents long since expired, several companies around the world compete with the current Fulton Bellows Company, but for the most part, the seamless metal bellows invented by Fulton set the standard for the industry.

From the inception of the National Aeronautics and Space Administration (NASA), its engineers have relied on Fulton's invention. Two of their most vexing problems were providing drinking water for astronauts in space and dampening the tremendous vibrations generated by the large Saturn V rocket engines.

Engineers at the company worked with NASA engineers to design a system that contained special bellows-operated valves that forced the flow of water out of its storage containers in the weightlessness of space, thereby making the water accessible for the astronauts. As part of the same project, NASA engineers used bellows as seals in the device that collected the space vehicle's wastewater. The problem of troublesome vibration in the piping complex near the huge rocket engines was relieved by the flexibility of multiple metal bellows.

The February 19, 1999 issue of the *Tennessee Star Journal* included a discussion on how the company "also worked closely with scientists developing the Space Shuttle program. In fact, without a bellows-inspired device today, there would be no drinking water on Space Shuttle flights." The article went on, "While history texts have relegated Weston Fulton's

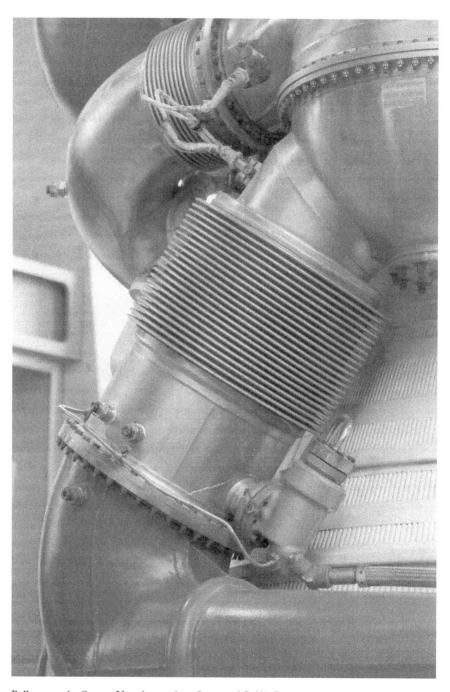

Bellows on the Saturn V rocket engine. *Courtesy of Robbie Bottoms.*

inventions to footnotes or industrial trivia, the employees, both past and present, have preserved everything they can about the man and the company he founded."

The following excerpt from a NASA press release describes some of the equipment that was used on the Apollo 8 mission:

> *The liquid hydrogen is stored in an insulated tank at less than minus 423 degrees Fahrenheit. Hydrogen from the tank is supplied to the J-2 engine turbo pump by a vacuum-jacketed, low pressure, 10-inch duct. This duct is capable of flowing 80 pounds per second at a transfer pressure of 28 psia. The duct is located in the aft tank side wall above the common bulkhead joint. Bellows in this duct compensate for engine gimbaling, manufacturing tolerances, and thermal motions.*

A similar NASA report described equipment on the Space Shuttle:

> *Two Freon coolant loops transport excess heat from the water/Freon interchanger, fuel cell heat exchanger, and payload heat exchanger....Each loop has a pump package consisting of two pumps and an accumulator. A metal bellows accumulator is pressurized with gaseous nitrogen to provide a positive pressure on the pumps and permit thermal expansion in the coolant loop. When the bellows is fully extended, approximately 80 pounds of Freon is in the accumulator.*

THE PROPOSED LUNAR WORM

The concept of a lunar worm shows the fascination aeronautical engineers have always had for metal bellows. In the mid-1960s, the Moon was still far away, but engineers were hard at work trying to come up with ways to explore its surface while dealing with its harsh environment and rough terrain. Philco Corporation, a NASA contractor, proposed in 1966 the use of a Lunar Worm Planetary Roving Vehicle. A large, unmanned bellows could be used to "inch" its way over the lunar surface.

The feasibility study presented to NASA by Philco engineers described variations of the proposed vehicle:

> *The concept wherein the bottom surface of the vehicle moves in the form of a traveling wave similar to the motion used by snakes and centipedes*

appears to be potentially the most versatile. It is capable of moderate to high speeds over rough terrain with a smoother ride and less vehicle bounce, good maneuverability, good propulsive efficiency, better ability to climb obstacles and to bridge crevices. It can be designed with a very low footprint pressure for use over a wide variety of surfaces, including even fluid-like soils through which it is capable of swimming.

Another concept envisioned the use of a double-acting bellows, which is a variation of rib-walking, where adjacent ribs contacting the surface are 180 degrees out of phase, appears quite suitable for unmanned vehicles with regard to simplicity, ease of deployment, weight and power requirements, but the ride tends to be rough, and ability to clear obstacles is somewhat limited. A version of this concept can be designed which is within the present state-of-the-art of metal bellows technology.

An extension-contraction bellows concept, wherein the vehicle alternately shortens and lengthens and propulsion is derived from asymmetry built into the lower surface, is the simplest concept considered but also requires the most power because of friction in sliding over the terrain. It is restricted in footprint loading and maneuverability but is uniquely suited for incorporation of a novel solar-mechanical energy transfer system, which holds some promise as a lightweight, inexpensive means for supplying mechanical energy for propulsion.

To say this device was never used is an understatement. It does, however, show the high regard that the bellows has always maintained with the people involved in solving the many problems associated with space exploration.

THE BELLOWS IN TROUBLE

Although bellows have figured prominently in helping engineers at NASA solve some of their most troublesome problems, the path has not always been a smooth one. The bellows itself created a serious problem on one of the missions and was the center of a series of investigations.

During the test flight of the second Saturn V vehicle, one of the J-2 engines on the second stage malfunctioned, causing the engine to shut down early. Then, during that same flight, the J-2 engine on the third stage failed to restart in Earth orbit.

During a series of test firings, as engineers tried to determine what was causing the problem, it was discovered that some of the hydrogen delivery lines had developed leaks. After several weeks, the investigators determined that the anomalies were the result of flow-induced vibration fatigue failures of the metal bellows.

An excerpt from NASA engineer H.J. Bandgren gives a flavor of the technical language as the bellows were undergoing scrutiny. "When the vortex-shedding frequency of the bellows coincides with one of the longitudinal resonant frequencies of the bellows, a strong bellows vibration may result." It was decided that the problem could be solved by installing flow liners inside the bellows and adding more damping around the entire bellows system.

MAVEN: NASA's Mars Mission

The MAVEN (Mars Atmospheric and Volatile Evolution) Mission launched from Cape Canaveral, Florida, on November 18, 2013, and went into Mars orbit on September 22, 2014, after a ten-month-long journey. The spacecraft, weighing 5,410 pounds, began its one-year primary science mission on November 16, 2014, as it carried out regular observations of the Martian upper atmosphere, ionosphere and solar wind interactions using nine scientific instruments. The mission is currently providing measurements of the Martian atmosphere to help understand dramatic climate change on the red planet over its history.

In December 2014, scientists announced that the MAVEN instruments had detected two unexpected surprises: a dust cloud was found between 90 and 190 miles above the surface, and a bright ultraviolet glow in the planet's northern hemisphere was observed.

Scientists have believed for some time that Mars once had a somewhat dense atmosphere and that surface water was present. Further, scientists believe that most of the planet's atmosphere has been lost to space. MAVEN produced evidence that the planet's climate could possibly have supported life in some form before transitioning to its present-day cold and dry condition.

The MAVEN spaceship was powered by a rocket manufactured by Pratt and Whitney Company. Bellows that were made by the company are part of the system that controls its fuel system.

AT SEA

For several years, U.S. Coast Guard cutters have contained numerous valves that were manufactured by the company. Most of those that were used by the cutters were "hot chamber" types, whereby the medium to be controlled flows directly over a gas-charged bellows. The bellows expands or contracts as necessary to correctly position the valve plug in relation to the valve seat, thus providing automatic temperature control. A typical application of this is the regulation of steam in order to achieve the desired temperature of hot water used in the ship's dining facility.

The U.S. Navy uses large valves built by the company that have thermal wax charges that are placed in contact with the controlled medium. A typical application for these large valves is controlling the temperature of cooling water systems of standby electric generators on nuclear submarines and aircraft carriers.

Bellows-powered thermal actuators. *Author's collection.*

ROBERTSHAW
SUBSAFE REGULATOR 98587-C1

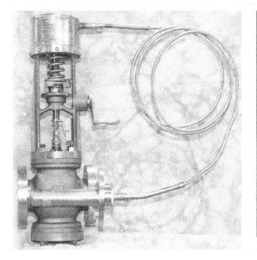

Submarine-qualified controls. *Author's collection.*

MEDICAL APPLICATIONS

Neither doctors nor patients see the bellows that is inside the machine that keeps patients' blood at the required temperature during open-heart surgery. The heat exchanger often used by manufacturers of cardiopulmonary heat exchangers has as its main element a stainless-steel bellows. Because of its many convolutions, the bellows offers a large area for heat dissipation in a small space. The blood is directed through the outside convolutions of the bellows, which is located inside a housing made of polycarbonate. The heat exchangers can be used for hypothermic (abnormally cold blood temperature) or normothermic (normal blood temperature) applications.

Nearly every hospital room and doctor's examining room in the United States has an instrument that is used for vacuuming obstructions from a patient's throat and lungs. Most of these instruments contain a metal bellows. The bellows causes a connected dial to indicate in millimeters of mercury the amount of vacuum being drawn. The doctor can then choose the proper amount of vacuum to use.

For several years, manufacturers of medical devices have either used or have attempted to use bellows in several other applications, including

MRI scanners, blood pressure circulators (indicate blood flow efficiency), hemostatic powder applicators (used to stop bleeding), cochlear devices, implantable instruments and invasive intravascular tubing.

AUTOMATIC PARACHUTE DEPLOYMENT

A fighter pilot who has to parachute from an altitude of more than twenty-five thousand feet will likely not survive because of hypoxia, or the lack of oxygen, unless there is some way for the pilot to get to a supply of oxygen. One method involves allowing the pilot to free-fall to fourteen thousand feet. Falling at the rate of approximately 120 miles per hour, the tumbling pilot quickly reaches the level where oxygen is plentiful, and the parachute automatically deploys. A metal bellows manufactured by the company, with a predictable spring rate that has been precisely calculated, senses the rapidly increasing barometric pressure as the pilot descends and the air pressure around him becomes higher. This pressure change causes the bellows to compress, just as Fulton's early barometers and altimeters had, and the subsequent movement triggers a switch that causes the parachute to deploy.

The navy describes the operation of its automatic parachute system as follows:

1. *The arming pin is pulled, which will allow the assembly to fire at or below a preset altitude.*
2. *A latch and the aneroid (bellows) assembly lock the ripcord release.*
3. *As the pilot free-falls, increasing barometric pressure causes the bellows to contract.*

Jim Otto, retired company bellows design engineer. *Author's collection.*

4. *As the preset altitude is reached, the bellows contracts sufficiently to release the latch from the firing mechanism.*
5. *The firing pin strikes a cartridge.*
6. *The cartridge fires.*
7. *A piston is moved forward, pulling a cable, which is attached to locking pins.*
8. *With the removal of the locking pins, the parachute is automatically deployed.*

"STAR WARS" AND THE COMPANY

In a television address to the nation on March 23, 1983, President Reagan announced his proposed Space Defense Initiative. It would include a missile defense system in outer space that would have the ability to destroy incoming enemy missiles. The president said, "Tonight, consistent with our obligations of the ABM Treaty and recognizing the need for closer consultation with our allies, I'm taking an important first step. I am directing a comprehensive and intense effort to define a long-term research and development program to begin to achieve our ultimate goal of eliminating the threat posed by strategic nuclear missiles. This could pave the way for arms control measures to eliminate the weapons themselves." Reagan later said, "I call upon the scientific community who gave us nuclear weapons to turn their great talents to the cause of mankind and world peace to give us the means of rendering these nuclear weapons impotent and obsolete." The president's proposal came about largely due to his strong distaste for the doctrine that was known at the time as "mutually assured destruction" doctrine, or MAD.

The plans called for a system that would protect the United States from Soviet intercontinental ballistic missiles. The conceptual design called for high-performance computer systems, lasers, particle beam weapons and the deployment of four thousand satellites in low Earth orbit. The individual components that would be required for the novel program had not yet been researched and developed.

In the 1980s, before President Reagan's announcement, the fact that research was being conducted on such a program was a badly kept secret. The government said it did not exist, but the rumors and leaks ultimately proved this to be untrue.

Needing a method for repositioning their satellites to accurately launch missiles to destroy enemy missiles, representatives from the Defense Department asked to meet with company personnel, as they had done so many times in the past. It is now known that bellows assemblies, made from inconel to withstand the very high pressures inside the storage tanks, would be the device used to maneuver the satellites to their required positions by expelling nitrogen into space, thus making use of the "opposite and equal force" law of physics. The bellows was part of a valve assembly, with specifications so stringent that the seating components of the valve assembly required a polished mirror-like finish.

Unfortunately, the company lost the initial contract to a competitor's better pricing. However, when the competitor could not perform to the satisfaction of Defense Department personnel, a contract was quickly negotiated between the Defense Department's contractor Aerojet Tech Systems and the company. With the time that had been lost, the program to incorporate the bellows assembly was significantly behind schedule.

Concerned Defense Department personnel asked for permission to send a representative to company facilities every day to physically check on the status of their order. On one occasion, the government representative waited an entire day for the assemblies to be removed from a seasoning process in a bake-out oven so he could fulfill his orders and physically look at them.

The space program was initially named "Smart Rocks" but was changed to "Brilliant Pebbles" by the late 1980s. For the design engineers, most government officials and finally the press, it became universally known as "Star Wars."

In Reykjavik, Iceland, during one of several summit meetings between President Reagan and Soviet leader Michail Gorbachev, White House chief of staff Donald Regan reported:

> *Gorbachev stated, "OK, let's not even leave a hundred missiles, let's abolish them completely and go for the zero option." This came as a shock. Reagan hit the table and said, "Well, why didn't you say that in the first place? That's exactly what I wanna do, and if you wanna do away with all the weapons, I'll agree to do away with all the weapons!" "All weapons?" Gorbachev asked. "Of course, we'll do away with all weapons! Good! That's great! Now, now we have an agreement!" Gorbachev answered, "Yes, but you must confine the Space Defense Initiative to the laboratory!" "No, I won't," said Reagan. "No way! SDI continues! I told you that! I am never going to give up SDI."*

The Soviet Union imploded, and by 1991, the Cold War had somewhat come to an end. The SDI would remain part of America's national defense

TENNESSEE
DIVISION NEWS
Number 226   March 1989
Knoxville Edition

Space Based Interceptor
Advanced Liquid Axial Stage

'Star Wars' and Tennessee Division
FROM WWI ANTI-SUB TO SDI DEFENSE
The Sylphon Bellows and Associated Products Have Been There

The flexible, seamless metal bellows invented by Weston M. Fulton in Knoxville at the turn of the century was designed to measure atmospheric pressure changes. Variations of the design have been applied to countless purposes — in construction, in the home, in industry, for automobiles and in aeronautics. There has also been a military side to its usage.

The first military application was made in WWI depth bombs to either stabilize their chosen flotation level or to cause them to explode at a selected depth, both in relation to the surrounding water pressure.

Seventy-five to 80 years later, the "Sylphon" bellows has a place in the United States' latest military frontier — the Strategic Defense Initiative. Our customer, Aerojet Tech Systems Company, is building a Space Based Interceptor prototype. The bellows assembly supplied on a critical shipment basis will be involved in the intitial response movement made by the interceptor to destroy launched enemy nuclear warheads.

The customer is most appreciative of the special and extra efforts of sales, engineering, supervision, and those of the hourly work force involved in supplying the prototype bellows as and when

needed. (See Tom Moon's column on Just-In-Time.)

Bellows remain a "viable" product for the Tennessee Division because of the possible precise linear movement in relation to temperature and/or pressure changes, and slight offset capability in misalignment applications, and as a flexible shield, barrier or container in others; and because of our work force's ability to design and manufacture them to exact specifications and materials requirements.

(Thanks for the lead and assist on this article given by Sales Application Engineer Rodger Lowe.)

Company's newsletter. *Author's collection.*

strategy for only two more years. During that time, NASA launched a space probe called *Clementine* that used Brilliant Pebbles technology as it mapped the entire surface of the Moon.

Because of the secrecy involved, it was impossible for company personnel to know for sure if the bellows guidance system was actually used on the *Clementine* mission. It can be assumed, however, that Weston Fulton's bellows went to work in space again.

111

By the late 1980s, the Defense Department shifted its focus to conventional-type missiles. Even though the successful $80 million *Clementine* space mission easily qualified Brilliant Pebbles as a potential defense system, it was not enough to save the program, and it was canceled in 1993.

DISNEY WORLD MONORAIL

The monorail trains at Disney World, in a novel approach to transportation, have rubber tires rather than steel ones. The trains carry an average of 150,000 riders daily. Although the trains have a maximum speed of seventy miles per hour, the maximum speed allowed at the park is forty miles per hour, and certain parts of the rail system limit the speed to fifteen miles per hour. The monorail tires are commercial-grade truck tires that have an estimated average lifespan of more than sixty thousand miles.

On June 6, 1985, the rear car of one of Disney World's monorail trains that was en route from Epcot Station to the Transportation and Ticket Center caught fire, trapping several passengers inside. Fortunately, the passengers were able to kick out the windows and scramble onto the car's roof. From there, they were rescued by members of the Reedy Creek Fire Department. Seven of the passengers were hospitalized with smoke inhalation. Since this incident, the park has installed a window that can be opened from the inside and a trapdoor that leads to the roof in each car.

In the ensuing investigation, the fire department determined that the fire was caused by a flat tire that ignited as it was dragged along the supporting concrete beam. Disney World's engineers immediately started searching for a way to prevent the recurrence of such a problem.

Coincidentally, the company had been working for several months with Scoville-Schrader Company as it developed a sensor for automobile and truck tires that would indicate to the operator when their tires were flat or underinflated. Disney World purchased some of the new sensors and installed them inside all the tires on the monorail trains.

About two years later, the management at Scoville-Schrader Company decided to stop manufacturing the sensors. Because the sensors were so important to the operation of the monorails, Disney World purchased all manufacturing and marketing rights to the device, and if it had wished, it could have been the exclusive worldwide distributor of the product. However, a few years later, the bellows-operated tire sensors at Disney World were replaced by sensors using electronic strain gauge technology.

Monorail at Disney World. *Courtesy of Suzanne Henry.*

Left: Ed Dexter, retired company bellows design engineer. *Author's collection.*

Right: Dan Harrison, retired company master electrician. *Author's collection.*

BELLOWS-OPERATED GAS LIFT VALVES
USED IN OIL WELLS

Production from oil wells is reduced as the amount of oil in the well decreases. To prolong the productivity of the well, several methods can be used to increase production—at least temporarily. A popular method is a system that includes a gas lift valve, whereby nitrogen at pressures as high as 5,000 PSI is pumped into a tube that has a fitting below the surface of the oil in the well. The gas lift valve furnishes the gas pressure that forces the oil to the surface.

The gas lift valve has multiple chambers. The top chamber is filled with pressurized natural gas through a small valve that is like those on automobile tires. When the desired pressure is reached, the valve is sealed. In the second chamber is a gas-operated bellows that is charged to open a valve at a specified pressure in the nitrogen supply line. The internal pressure in the chamber forces the bellows against the valve seat. Three-ply monel bellows are used because of the high pressure and hostile environment they must withstand.

When the gas lift valve is lowered to a point under the surface of the remaining oil in the well, the lower chamber is exposed to the well pressure at that depth. The pressure differential between that pressure and that of the gas being pumped into the well forces the oil to be "lifted" to the surface.

Experts in the field estimate that this method or a similar one is used in more than 20 percent of all oil wells worldwide.

PANIC IN CHERNOBYL

On the morning of April 28, 1986, extremely high radiation levels set off sirens at a nuclear power plant in Forsmark, Sweden. Frightened and concerned technicians at the plant notified authorities, and an urgent search was launched in an attempt to determine the source of the radiation. Two days later, it was learned that the source was a nuclear reactor accident in Chernobyl, Russia, which was located 620 miles away.

The world would soon learn that at 1:21 a.m. on April 26, 1986, the no. 4 reactor at the Chernobyl Nuclear Plant near the Russian city of Pripyat experienced a nuclear explosion. The disaster was rated at 7—the highest severity on the International Nuclear Event Scale. Only the 2011 disaster at the Fukishima Nuclear Plant in Japan shares this top rating.

The problem started during a test to see if the reactor would be safe during a short power outage, at which time, the necessary pumps for furnishing cooling water were inoperable. After the intended short power outage, it took about sixty seconds for the diesel engines to get to full speed and furnish power to the cooling pumps. Unfortunately, this planned short shutdown set events in motion that the inexperienced technicians could not cope with. The fact that this event took place during shift change likely added to the confusion.

About twenty minutes after the fire started in the reactor, several fire engines arrived to fight the fire that was thought to only be an electrical-type fire. Lieutenant Volodymyr Pravyk, the fireman in charge, said, "We didn't know it was the reactor....No one had told us." Pravyk died on May 9 from radiation sickness.

Grigori Khmel, a driver of one of the fire engines described what happened:

> *We arrived there at ten or fifteen minutes to two in the morning and saw graphite scattered around. Misha asked, "Is that graphite?" I kicked it away, but one of the drivers in another truck picked it up and said that it was hot....We didn't know much about radiation. Even those who worked there had no idea. There was no water left in the trucks. Misha filled a cistern, and we aimed the water at the top. Then those boys went up to the roof—Vashchik, Kolya and Volodymyr Pravyk. They went up the ladder, and I never saw them again.*

Another fireman, Anatoli Zakharov, added, "I remember joking that we all would be lucky if we were alive in the morning, because there must be an incredible amount of radiation here. Of course, we knew that we should have never gone near the reactor. But it was a moral obligation—our duty. We were like kamikazes."

Reactor crew chief Aleksandr Akimov stayed with his crew until morning as they attempted to pump water into the reactor. None of them wore any protective gear, and nearly all of them, including Akimov, died within three weeks.

The explosion released a large amount of energy, and the reactor core had ruptured. A fire in the core burned for nine days and released a considerable amount of airborne radioactive contamination. About 75 percent of the radiation landed on the nearby city of Pripyat.

At 11:00 a.m. on April 27, buses came to evacuate citizens from Pripyat. An announcement to those affected read:

For the attention of the residents of Pripyat! The city council informs you that due to the accident at Chernobyl Power Station in the city of Pripyat, the radioactive conditions in the vicinity are deteriorating. The Communist Party, its officials and the armed forces are taking necessary steps to combat this. Nevertheless, with the view to keep people as safe and healthy as possible, the children being top priority, we need to temporarily evacuate the citizens in the nearest towns in the Kiev region....It is highly advisable to take your documents, some vital personal belongings, and a certain amount of food, just in case, with you....All houses will be guarded by the police during the evacuation period. Comrades leaving your residence temporarily, please make sure you have turned off the lights, electrical equipment and water and shut the windows. Please keep calm and orderly in the process of this short-term evacuation.

In the initial explosion, thirty-one workers lost their lives; twenty-five more died over the next few weeks from radiation exposure. Hundreds of thousands of Ukrainians, Russians and Belarusians who were within twenty-five miles of the disaster were forced to abandon their homes. It was estimated that 3 million people in Belarus alone lived in the contaminated zone.

During the nine days that it took to extinguish the fire at Chernobyl, approximately six hundred helicopter pilots risked their lives as they dumped about five thousand tons of lead, sand and clay on the site. Later, the entire building was completely enclosed in concrete.

Faced with this sudden dilemma, and with pressure from its own people and the world, the Russian government desperately needed to monitor the radiation levels to determine the distance its people needed to be evacuated to. Realizing it needed expert assistance, the Russian government contacted ORTEC Incorporated, an Oak Ridge, Tennessee firm, and placed an emergency order for several dozen radiation detectors it manufactured.

For several years, the company had been providing bellows to ORTEC for use as special seals in their radiation detectors. The normal delivery time was ten to twelve weeks. Because the bellows had the longest lead time of any of the detector's components, ORTEC personnel requested an emergency meeting with the company. Representatives of the company went to Oak Ridge for an emergency Saturday morning meeting, at which time, ORTEC immediately placed an order for bellows.

Realizing the enormity of the situation, the company representatives promised to produce the bellows in just ten days. This meant placing much of the other work in the bellows production department on hold while working extra shifts. Ten days later, the completed bellows were delivered to ORTEC in this author's company car. The detectors were then assembled and quickly shipped to the Russians.

THE BELLOWS ATTEMPTS TO HELP THE "WORST CAR IN HISTORY"

The Yugoslavian-made Yugo automobile shows up on most "top fifty worst cars in history" lists, and most of these magazine articles describe the many shortcomings of the sad little car. After conceding that it was competitively priced at the time for about $4,000, its undesirable traits are then usually pointed out. Marketed in the United States between 1985 and 1992, it was generally found to be unreliable and dangerously underpowered—it took fourteen seconds to reach sixty miles per hour. Making things worse, the timing belt on the fifty-five-horsepower engine had to be replaced every forty thousand miles.

Most other automobiles that were being built at the time had fuel-injected engines, making them impervious to changes in elevation. However, the inexpensive Yugo still had an old-fashioned carburetor, which meant the car became almost helpless when it was exposed to high elevations because the lean/rich ratio or air/fuel mixture was different than when the car was driven at lower elevations.

This problem had been solved for airplanes and other automobiles many years before by Weston Fulton's bellows-operated device that acted on changes in barometric pressure. So, once again, Fulton's bellows were asked to automatically control the fuel/air mixture in the little car, thereby helping it negotiate higher elevations more easily. Tens of thousands of bellows were furnished for this application until the car's inability to pass U.S. environmental standards curtailed its market, and unrest in the former Yugoslavia finally brought about the end of the Yugo.

TSUNAMI AND SCRAM VALVES

The world watched in horror as tsunami waves caused by the shock of an earthquake swept across a wide area of northern Japan on March 11, 2011. In the affected area, Tokyo Electric and Power Company operated the Fukushima Nuclear Power Plant.

Strikingly similar to the disaster that had occurred in Chernobyl in 1986, electric power for the pumps that furnished cooling water for the reactors was lost. During the next few days, rising heat in the core of the reactor caused the fuel rods to overheat and partially melt down. Resulting explosions and fires caused the release of airborne radiation.

Workers started pumping seawater and boric acid into the reactors in an attempt to slow the fires and mitigate the radiation that was being released. Similar to the actions taken at Chernobyl, water from fire trucks and helicopters was constantly dumped on the reactors for days.

A no-fly zone of twenty miles was later established. Citizens were immediately evacuated in a land radius of fifteen miles from the accident site. The land evacuation distance was soon raised to a radius of twenty miles. Approximately forty-seven thousand people were ordered to leave their homes. Others who lived near the evacuation zone also fled. All were encouraged to stay indoors as much as possible.

Almost lost in early reports by the news media was the fact that the nuclear power plant's SCRAM system had performed properly. The valves that were over thirty years old worked as they had been designed. SCRAM control valves were manufactured by the company in the 1970s and sold to General Electric Company for use in these and many other nuclear installations. To maintain optimum working conditions, Robertshaw Controls Company (formerly part of the company) periodically replaces SCRAM valve parts in nuclear reactors built by General Electric Company in several countries.

SCRAM is an acronym for Safety Control Rod Axe Man, which generally refers to the emergency shutdown of a nuclear reactor. This term has been in use since the first nuclear reaction beneath a stadium in Chicago under the direction of Enrico Fermi. A man literally stood, ready with an ax, to cut a rope that would release the anti-reactivity material into the reactor.

At Fukushima, which has light water reactors, a different method was used for slowing down the nuclear fission. Chemicals that rapidly flow through pipes and valves start the "cooling down" process within a four-second period. Even though the SCRAM valves had performed as required, the loss of electricity to the pumps that furnished cooling water to the reactors led to this disaster that was second only to that of Chernobyl.

Aircraft Oxygen Applications

The flight attendant dutifully tells the passengers, "In the unlikely event we lose cabin pressure, oxygen masks will drop from the overhead compartment. Please place the mask on your own face and then on any children you might have with you." Neither the attendant nor the passengers see the bellows assembly that might sit unused in the airliner for years but is expected to work flawlessly when needed. Constantly sensing the cabin pressure, the bellows assembly instantly triggers the device that deploys the oxygen for the passengers' immediate use if the cabin pressure, which is normally maintained at the equivalent of ten thousand feet of altitude, reaches a pressure that is equal to fourteen thousand feet of altitude.

Bellows are used to sense barometric pressure in aircraft flying at very high altitudes. A bellows senses the atmospheric pressure and uses this information to regulate the fuel flow into jet engines.

Air moving through ducts of an aircraft is sometimes controlled by bellows sensors. Bellows are also used as flexible joints that are hermetically sealed to the aircraft cockpit instrument panel, allowing instrumentation outside the wall to be adjusted from inside the cockpit without loss of pressure.

Desert Storm: The Bellows Goes to War Again

As Desert Shield turned into Desert Storm in 1991, the company found itself in a crisis. Due to causes that will be described in the next chapter, there was deep concern among the company employees that they might not be able to provide replacement parts needed by the army, navy and air force.

At that time, a display was put together in the company's sales department that showed all the items that the company manufactured for the Defense Department. Because of security concerns, this display could not be shown to the public but was made purely for the benefit of the employees who might feel some pride in the contribution they made with their products.

The following is a partial list of the aircraft and missiles that had company-made bellows in their fuel or guidance systems during Desert Storm:

- F-14 air force fighter
- F-15 air force fighter
- F-16 air force fighter
- B-52 air force bomber
- various navy fighters
- various army helicopters
- Tomahawk missile
- Hell-Fire missile

F-18 Hornet fighter plane. *Courtesy of the U.S. Navy.*

Side Winder air-to-air missile. *Courtesy of the U.S. Navy.*

Additionally, company-provided valves or thermostats were in use on every aircraft carrier, destroyer, submarine and coast guard cutter deployed in the Persian Gulf theater. Many at the company realized that Americans would have been deeply concerned had they known how much the defense of the country was resting on a company that was in a weakened condition and possibly would be unable to respond to requests for replacement parts. Fortunately, the conflict ended in a few days, and parts were not needed.

14

THE COMPANY'S VARIED MARKET BASKET

By 1986, the company was approaching one hundred years of age. The concerted effort to vary the types of products it offered had paid off several times over, as it helped dampen the effects of numerous recessions. The products being manufactured could be placed in three main categories: (1) bellows and bellows assemblies; (2) automotive-related devices, such as engine thermostats, exhaust gas recirculation valves and pollution control valves; and (3) industrial controls consisting of items like temperature regulators, control valves, engine controls, pressure gauges and level controls.

The company's annual sales totaled about $90 million. Sales forecasts were showing expected sales within five years totaling $120 million, with an expected increase in the number of employees by about six hundred. A ceramic plaque with "#1" on it, indicating that the company had been the top division within all of Robertshaw Controls Company, had hung beside the general manager's office longer than anyone could remember.

Although this was among the most prosperous times the company had ever experienced, the bellows group in particular was feeling pressure from two different types of competitors. One that it had not faced before came from the rapid growth of electronics. With the advent of strain gauge technology, the sensing unit could be interfaced with a computer via an electronic circuit. The second new and strong competitive threat came from foreign suppliers. The emergence of a global market and a shrinking world due to wide-bodied aircraft, containerized ships and the availability of easy-to-use electronic communication allowed buyers in the United States to be more receptive to overtures from foreign suppliers. Three foreign firms that captured a sizable part of the American bellows business were Witzenmann (German), BOA (Swiss) and Kuse (Japanese).

Predictably, as more suppliers entered the market, those manufacturers that badly needed to raise their prices could not. In many cases, they were actually forced to reduce their prices. Profits fell precipitously for all of the bellows suppliers. This meant that various companies became more likely to raid the turf of their competitors, often quoting unreasonably low prices, thus starting a cycle of ruinous competition.

"Nothing to Worry About"

In 1986, employees at the company were told that after decades of owning the company, Reynolds Metals Company was selling it to a British leverage-buy-out firm. Employees were assured that there was nothing to worry about and that everything would be just as it was before. For the next three years, this was essentially true. However, with 1989 just a few days old, the situation started to change. Apparently, there was reason to worry after all.

The well-known nature of a leverage-buy-out company is to buy a firm and use its assets to buy another company and then use that company's assets to buy another company. They often have little or no interest in the success or failure of the businesses they have acquired along the way. This type of company needs to raise liquidity rapidly and often acquire a company to use its capital equipment as collateral in order to buy more firms to keep its operation going. The leverage involved often means that the inventory of a newly acquired firm will be drastically reduced without regard as to what is necessary to meet the needs of customers and, more importantly, retain them.

The constant insistence that the company reduce its inventory to the bone brought dire consequences. With total disregard to the requirements of its thousands of customers, the inventory of parts was slashed. Alarmingly, the purchases of the parts needed to fill the orders on hand were stopped. Shipments to customers came to a halt, invoices quit going out and checks stopped coming in to pay the salaries of the company's approximately 1,400 employees. Within weeks, valued customers became desperate when they could not get their shipments, and several faced bankruptcies because they, in turn, could not ship their products. Many threatened lawsuits, while others simply went about seeking replacement suppliers.

While some quality and delivery problems had occurred during the preceding few years, they were handled efficiently and caused little more than bumps in the road. The new owners of the company and their management style and philosophy, however, created chaotic conditions. While just-in-time delivery methods, continuous flow, customer-dedicated work areas and keeping little or no inventory on hand are good management techniques in general, for the company, they failed completely. This was largely because many of the products the company produced, although often demanding high unit prices, were sold in quantities that were too small to support those manufacturing techniques. "One size does not fit all" was proven once again.

The admonition in all college-level textbooks regarding the reduction of parts inventory is in general: "Lower the level of the water in the pond carefully, all the while looking for stumps. When a stump is found and removed, lower the water a little more." Sadly, this well-documented warning was ignored.

Hundreds of customers who had been promised ten- to twelve-week deliveries were suddenly told that they would receive their bellows assemblies or valves in twenty-six weeks. Some would learn that even this was not possible. A judge representing the U.S. Air Force, and Barksdale Air Force Base in particular, issued a show cause letter asking why the company should not be sued for failure to deliver bellows assemblies for their B-52 bombers, since they had been promised a ten- to twelve-week delivery and had not received them in thirteen months.

Inside Job

In this time of confusion, and with morale of the employees at an all-time low, the employees' credit union was robbed. Just as they had done for several years, the managers of the credit union had amassed tens of thousands of extra dollars in order to cash vacation checks for the workers, who were going on a two-week company-wide vacation. With the cloud of uncertainty hanging over the employees, robbers cleaned out their credit union, safe and all.

Sometime after midnight, while the guard was making his regular rounds, which took him to the back of the plant for about an hour, the robbers boldly drove into the underground parking garage and jimmied a door open that led to the front offices of the facility. They operated a freight elevator that normally no longer stopped on the second floor (where the credit union was located). The opening for the elevator on that floor had been enclosed with sheetrock and painted. Most employees did not even know that there was an elevator behind the wall.

The robbers stopped the elevator at the blank wall on the second floor and broke through the sheetrock, located about one hundred feet from the credit union office. They broke into the office and, using a dolly or something similar, they transported the safe back to the elevator and exited the building. The guard never heard or saw a thing.

The blasted-open safe was found a few days later in North Carolina. Even though it was obvious that at least one of the robbers had been familiar with the elevator situation—therefore indicating that it was an inside job—no one was ever charged with the crime.

Hard Times

The path to the essential destruction of the company took less than six months. The proud and profitable company, where so many people had worked during the last one hundred years, was dying. A few desperate attempts were made to try to save the company. One idea was to offer all employees who were over fifty-five years of age an early retirement. Fifty-one of the most-skilled employees, including engineers and technicians, were paid $400 per month to simply go home. Ninety-six hourly workers were laid off at a time when the orders on hand were at an all-time high. Much of the $31 million in order backlog—much of it months late—would never be shipped. Order cancellations would take care of that.

Many knowledgeable company personnel, realizing the hopelessness of the situation, essentially gave up. As many as possible found other jobs. Their best customers were then lost, and many others were getting company competitors tooled up to become suppliers. Among their lost customers was their largest prize of all: Ford Motor Company. This one was, perhaps, the harshest blow of all. For years, the company had been Ford's sole source of thermostats, EGR valves and PCV valves. Reluctantly, and after several warnings for poor delivery and quality issues, Ford Motor Company no longer used the company as a supplier. Engineers and buyers at Ford had been busy during the several months prior, spending millions of dollars to tool up other suppliers.

The leverage-buy-out-company essentially lost all interest in the company, which it had never made an attempt to understand. It was ready to move on.

SPLINTERED APART AND THE BIG MOVE

The leverage-buy-out firm moved the automotive group to Mexico, where it was promptly sold. It was then moved to Indiana and is only a fraction of the size it once was. A small part of the industrial control group was moved to Maryville, Tennessee, where it is still manufacturing control valves, temperature regulators and some level controls.

An investment group borrowed $36 million from a bank and bought what was left of the company—the bellows operation. The new owners tried to manufacture bellows in the large facility that had once been used to produce all of the company's products. The monthly payments on such a large loan were so burdensome that within two years, the new owners had no choice but file for Chapter 11 bankruptcy protection.

The bankruptcy court referee solicited bidders for the company. The single offer that was received came from a Chattanooga-based capital investment firm that specialized in breathing life back into troubled businesses. Using a legal vehicle called a "stalking horse," it put together an offer that totaled about $6 million. The court accepted the offer, and the new owners made plans to move to a smaller facility within a year. With manageable loan payments, it was in a much better position to succeed. The new company was called the same name it was called eighty years prior: Fulton Bellows Company.

The bolts holding the heavy presses groaned as they were removed from the concrete floor. Most had been in place for more than fifty years. Day after day, trucks hauled the equipment that had been accumulated over more than a century to east Knoxville's Forks-of-the River Industrial Park. The new facility did not have space for everything, so thousands of tools and other pieces of equipment were sold at auction for prices little above their scrap value.

The leverage-buy-out firm still owned the property and decided it was in its best economic interest to demolish the buildings. Surprisingly, at that time, the *Ulster-Scot* newspaper in Ulster, Scotland, the area from which the Fultons had emigrated in 1735, reported:

> *The last link to one of America's greatest entrepreneurs, scientists and industrialists was destroyed recently in Knoxville, Tennessee. Few today have heard of Weston Miller Fulton, but one of his inventions continues to play an intricate role in just about every facet of people's daily lives the globe over. With the destruction of the Fulton home and now the bellows plant, the memory of one of America's great men fades.*

Sign in front of the present-day company facility. *Author's collection.*

Left: David Counts, current company bellows design engineer. *Author's collection.*

Right: Tina Holloway, company director of engineering. *Author's collection.*

The article went on to tell of Fulton's ancestors emigrating from County Down in the seventeenth century and to describe Fulton's achievements. With the story, the newspaper ran a photograph of Fulton's snow-covered Westcliff mansion and a caption, "Westcliff home from a 1930s Christmas card from the family."

Since the company has moved to its new quarters, it has bought two other bellows manufacturers, and the company itself has been purchased twice. Every day, thousands of metal bellows are being made. Even though Fulton's invention is over 115 years old, it is still used extensively in the fields of manufacturing, petroleum, defense, aerospace and medicine. In spite of all the twists and turns that have occurred in the past few years, Fulton's "sylph" has survived.

UNIVERSITY COMMONS

So, a cold slab was all that was left on the property of the once-proud company. It was a sad reminder of the pillage caused by the acquisition of the company in 1986. After several years of disuse, an announcement in the *Knoxville News-Sentinel* on November 24, 2011, indicated that a change was being planned. Reporter Josh Flory wrote that developers were working with clients such as Publix and Wal-Mart to anchor a mall that would include several smaller stores. The mall would be called University Commons.

In deference to Fulton and his original building, the developers decided that the mall would have the look and feel of a turn-of-the-century factory. The smokestack that had stood on the property for one hundred years was left to tower over the structure. Further, the architectural concept made use of stone, brick and ornamental steel throughout the design. Adding to the charm and staying with the early

The writer in front of the murals in University Commons. *Author's collection.*

twentieth-century theme, a working old-fashioned train station was planned at an entrance to the mall.

The well-laid plans of the developers all came true, and the stores opened to much fanfare. Eight-foot-tall photographs of Fulton, his inventions and his previous factory were placed on the walls of the entrances to the Publix and Wal-Mart stores. While University Commons no longer has Wal-Mart as a tenant, Publix, with its vintage Fulton-related photographs, and several other smaller shops continue to flourish.

15

THE FULTON FAMILY TODAY

The Fulton family lived in Westcliff through the Great Depression and World War II, until Weston's death in 1946. With her husband gone, Barbara decided that the mansion was an extravagance and sold it in 1947 for $85,000. Under the sales agreement, Barbara retained possession of the house until the end of that summer.

In October 1947, Barbara, her aged mother and her youngest daughter, Mary, moved to 3559 Iskagna Drive. In her later years, Barbara moved into Knoxville's Shannondale Retirement Community.

Westcliff was later bought for $110,000 by a Catholic order, the Sisters of Mercy, which renamed it Marycliff and placed an illuminated cross on its tower. For a time, the house was used as a rest home and dormitory for nurses who were in training at St. Mary's Memorial Hospital.

Sister Annunciata, a hospital administrator, said at the time, "The duty of training nurses is one of the most important activities of the Sisters of Mercy. Marycliff and its lovely surroundings, swimming pool, tennis court, etc., will add to the recreational and cultural functions always so essential to the professional nurse."

A few years later, Westcliff was sold again, and for the next several years, it was in gradual decline. Most of the opulent mansion was demolished in 1968 to make room for a condominium complex called, appropriately enough, Westcliff Condominiums. The original guardhouse and its watchtower still stand at the entrance to the upscale condominium complex. Still matching the architecture of the former Fulton home, the guardhouse is covered with Crab Orchard stone and stucco. Its tile roof matches the roof that was on the original mansion. The guardhouse alone is large enough to accommodate a family of five and has been constantly occupied since it was built.

The developers of the condominiums retained one side room and an exterior corridor of the original home. The room and its adjoining corridor, with its impressive arched galleries, serve to remind visitors of the glory days when the mansion was the talk of the western part of Knoxville and a big part of the Fulton legacy.

The nicely decorated single room is now rented to organizations for things like conferences and reunions. It also serves as the clubhouse for the condominiums. Just inside the front wall, in a prominent place, is a picture of the once-proud mansion. The remaining corridor with the Romanesque arches is often reserved for weddings.

A six-foot-tall brick wall surrounded the property for approximately half a mile. It was reminiscent of the walled cities of Europe, and much of the wall still stands. The small portion that is left of the mansion still sits atop the very highest of the nearby hills. That is the way Weston Fulton would have wanted it.

THE LIVES OF HIS CHILDREN

Weston Miller Fulton Jr., the Fulton's oldest child, was born on July 21, 1911. He died after an automobile accident on January 20, 1929, and was buried in the family plot in Highland Memorial Cemetery. The family donated their house to the University of Tennessee in his memory. The school acknowledged this gift by installing, in its new Student Health Facility, a bronze plaque and a commemorative sign along with a stained-glass window from the house that was razed to make room for a new student union building.

Barbara "Boo" Alexander Fulton was born on July 7, 1915. She aspired to be an actress and went to New York City to audition for several acting parts. After she did not land any major roles, her father financed a Broadway show so his daughter's dream could come true. The show, in which she was a costar, was only moderately successful. However, Boo did marry her leading man, Bruce Gentle. Several newspapers at the time had full-page pictures of Barbara's trousseau. She went on to Hollywood, where she auditioned for the part of Scarlett O'Hara in the movie *Gone with the Wind*.

Top: Bronze plaque in the University of Tennessee Student Health Center. *Author's collection.*

Bottom: Commemorative sign in the university's Student Health Center. *Author's collection.*

Lighted stained-glass window from the Fulton-donated house. *Author's collection.*

Barbara's marriage did not last long, and she returned to Knoxville. She later starred in several local productions at the University of Tennessee's Carousel Theater. She married Fenton Gentry, with whom she had one child, Fenton Jr. Barbara died on September 13, 1999, at the age of eighty-four.

Robert William Fulton was born on July 3, 1918. He graduated from McCallie Prep School, the University of Tennessee and Harvard University. He served as an officer in the quartermaster corps of the army during World War II. He became a successful businessman in Knoxville. He married Margaret McCready on September 15, 1942. They had two children: Barbara Diane and Robert William Jr. Robert died on April 29, 2007, at the age of eighty-eight.

Jean "Jeannie" Hudson Fulton was born on July 27, 1924. She was named for her paternal grandmother, Mary Brown Hudson. She graduated from the University of Tennessee in 1945 and married her high school sweetheart, James C. Talley II, soon after he returned from the war. Their wedding was held in the garden at Westcliff, and the reception was held in the third-floor ballroom. Jean's sisters, Barbara and Mary, were two of her five attendants. The Talleys had two children: James C. Talley III and Katherine. Jean died on January 28, 2007, and was buried in the family plot in Highland Memorial Cemetery. She was eighty-two years old.

Mary Helen Fulton was born on October 30, 1929. She graduated from Bradford Junior College and the University of Tennessee. She initially married James R. Arnhart. They named their one son Weston Miller, after her father. Her second marriage was to Cluster Jefferson Hartley and took place on July 26, 1953. They had two children: Stuart Alexander and Cluster Jefferson Jr. They were named for their maternal grandmother and paternal grandfather, respectively. Mary died on July 26, 2008, in Tuscaloosa, Alabama, at the age of seventy-eight. She was buried in the Fulton family plot in Highland Memorial Cemetery. A passage from her obituary read, "She often spoke of her love for Tennessee, the beauty of the Smoky Mountains, and Old Rocky Top. This beautiful transplanted flower grew in the Alabama sunshine, and like all living things, has returned to earth to bloom once again in God's paradise." Mary's cousin Ruth Fulton Tiedemann, who now lives in Nebraska, once said, "I knew her quite well growing up. One of my fondest memories of her was watching her drive up the long driveway to Westcliff with a carload of teenagers and the top down while I was playing under the willow tree. I also remember her bringing her best friend, Connie Fowler, and others to my seventh birthday party."

In 2005, the Fulton's fourth child, Jean Talley, and her husband, James, established the Weston Miller Fulton Scholarship to honor the accomplishments of Jean's father. The Talleys included a bequest to the University of Tennessee's College of Electrical and Computer Science in their estate plans. At the time, Jean said, "My dad loved UT football and didn't miss a game for more than twenty-five years. When I was fifteen years old, he took me to the Rose Bowl. I have never forgotten that trip. My father was such a generous man. He gave so much to so many. I know he would be honored that we are presenting this gift to the university he loved so much."

University of Tennessee personnel have taken great care to ensure that the Fulton legacy continues. Recognizing his many contributions to the school, in 2012, the university announced plans to display Fulton-related artifacts in its new Student Health Facility. These artifacts included a stained- and leaded-glass window from the house that was donated by the Fulton family to the school, a large bronze plaque that was salvaged from the same house and an oil portrait of Weston Miller Fulton Jr.

Next to the portrait is a recognition plaque that acknowledges the Fultons' 1929 gift to the university and describes the many years that the house served

Fulton family's Grecian-style monument. *Author's collection.*

as the Student Infirmary and, later, the Student Counseling Center. The names of Weston, Barbara and their four children are then listed.

In describing Barbara's life, the *Knoxville News-Sentinel* reported that when Westcliff was finished, she "became a gracious chatelaine of the home, which was built at a cost of more than $500,000, exclusive of the spacious landscaped grounds." As the most expensive home in Knoxville,

Weston Miller Fulton. *Courtesy of the Fulton Family Collection.*

it was a showplace and the scene of many cheery social events.

With Weston gone, Barbara stayed away from public life and had no apparent interest in civic, patriotic or club groups. She had always loved to travel, and many of the furnishings and art pieces in the mansion were mementos from the family's trips abroad, especially from their travels to Italy and France. She retained the same interest in traveling to the very end. The art collection was especially valuable.

Barbara died on November 10, 1971, when she was eighty-one years old. She was buried beside Weston in their family plot.

Fulton's legacy is destined to continue for a very long time. Not only did his inventions help save lives and take them, but they also made it possible for people to automatically and comfortably control the temperature in their homes. The engineered bellows he invented were used on devices that went from the bottom of the ocean to the heights of skyscrapers, the Moon and Mars.

Today, engineers regularly come to the company for help solving their problems. As long as they do, the weatherman whose name is now largely forgotten will continue affecting mankind.

PATENTS ISSUED TO WESTON MILLER FULTON

June 18, 1903	No. 731354	Collapsible Vessel for Atmospheric Motors
June 30, 1903	No. 732627	Collapsible Vessel for Atmospheric Motors
Aug. 25, 1903	No. 737093	Automatic Clock Winding Mechanism
Dec. 22, 1903	No. 747409	Buffer
March 8, 1904	No. 754132	Storage Tank or Receptacle
June 14, 1904	No. 762299	Receptacle for Liquids
June 14, 1904	No. 762300	Oil Can
July 12, 1904	No. 764572	Motor
Aug. 9, 1904	No. 766820	Thermo-sensitive Device
Aug. 16, 1904	No. 767476	Air-Break
Oct. 11, 1904	No. 772034	Tension Device for Scales–Pressure Gauges
Oc. 11, 1904	No. 772035	Thermal Motor
Dec. 27, 1904	No. 778237	Winding Mechanism for Clocks
June 20, 1905	No. 792588	Atmospheric Motor
July 25, 1905	No. 795761	Atmospheric Pressure and Temperature Motor
Nov. 28, 1905	No. 805720	Collapsible Vessel

Jan. 23, 1906	No. 810403	Reservoir for Gasoline and Other Vapor Burners
July 3, 1906	No. 824858	Thermo-sensitive Device for Heat Motors–Laggin Jackets
Dec. 4, 1906	No. 837296	Electric Welding Apparatus
March 5, 1907	No. 846297	Process of Making Collapsible and Expansible Vessels
May 14, 1907	No. 853351	Electric Brazing Machine
July 2, 1907	No. 858507	Process of Electric Welding
May 12, 1908	No. 887084	Flexible Corrugated Wall
July 28, 1908	No. 894429	Valve and Valve Construction
Aug. 4, 1908	No. 894947	Heat Controlling Device
Sept. 1, 1908	No. 897730	Device for Utilizing the Motion of Flexible Diaphragm
Oct. 6, 1908	No. 900511	Damper Regulator
Nov. 10, 1908	No. 903465	Flexible Wall
Nov. 24, 1908	No. 904771	Electric Welding Machine
Dec. 29, 1908	No. 907771	Valve
Jan. 12, 1909	No. 909176	Damper Regulator
March 1909	No. 916140	Electric Brazing Apparatus
Aug. 9, 1910	No. 967010	Flexible Corrugated Metal Wall
March 28, 1911	No. 987712	Temperature Regulator
July 25, 1911	No. 998767	Heating System and System for Temperature Regulation
Nov. 12, 1912	No. 1044040	Air Valve for Steam Radiators
April 28, 1914	No. 1095100	Corrugated Metal Wall
May 12, 1914	No. 1096296	Flexible Tubular Corrugated Metal Wall
May 19, 1914	No. 1097123	Steam Boiler Attachment
June 30, 1914	No. 1102035	Automatic Tank Regulator
Dec. 21, 1915	No. 1165087	Carburetor

Jan. 25, 1916	No. 1169250	Shock Absorber for Water Pipes
March 14, 1916	No. 1175253	Quick Action Valve
June 6, 1916	No. 1186180	System of Temperature Regulation
Nov. 7, 1916	No. 1203601	Carburetor
Dec. 12, 1916	No. 1208130	Fluid Mixing Device
Feb. 27, 1917	No. 1217587	Cooling System for Internal Combustion Engines
Dec. 25, 1917	No. 1251214	Automatic Regulator
Dec. 31, 1918	No. 1289434	Valve
Feb. 4, 1919	No. 1293078	Process of Tempering Corrugated Walls
April 15, 1919	No. 1300717	Tank Regulator
Feb. 17, 1920	No. 1331100	Damper
March 20, 1920	No. 1332392	Dispensing Device
May 4, 1920	No. 1338916	Humidifying Device
May 18, 1920	No. 1340604	Means for Attaching Handles to Valve Stems
Aug. 10, 1920	No. 1349058	Heat Regulating Means
Nov. 9, 1920	No. 1358193	Ventilating Device
Nov. 16, 1920	No. 1358723	Temperature Regulator
Nov. 16, 1920	No. 1358947	Automobile Heating System
Jan. 11, 1921	No. 1364927	Automatic Thermostatic Safety Device–Radiator Dampers
July 12, 1921	No. 1384314	Speed Responsive Device
Jan. 30, 1923	No. 1443465	Automatic Radiator Curtain
March 9, 1926	No. 1576186	Thermostatically Operated Radiator Casing
Oct. 11, 1927	No. 1644775	Packless Valve
Nov. 1, 1927	No. 1647219	Receptacle for Discharging Fluids
Jan. 3, 1928	No. 1654585	Method and Apparatus for Drawing Tubes
May 8, 1928	No. 1668895	Expansible and Collapsible Receptacle

Oct. 23, 1928	No. 284137	*Appareil D'Etirage De Tubes* (Canadian)
Feb. 12, 1929	No. 1702047	Method and Appartus for Making Flexible Tubular Walls
April 16, 1929	No. 1709011	Extruded Tubular Wall and Method of Making Same
Oct. 18, 1932	No. 1882798	Manufacture of Tubular Corrugated Metal Walls
Aug. 21, 1934	No. 1970650	Method of Making Flexible Corrugated Tubular Walls
Sept. 19, 1939	No. 2173414	Feeder
April 22, 1941	No. 2239487	Medicine Cabinet
Oct. 31, 1944	No. 2361836	Stoker
Feb. 26, 1946	No. 2395732	Fuel Feeder
Feb. 26, 1946	No. 2395733	Rotary Burner

POSTHUMOUS PATENTS:

Aug. 26, 1947	No. 2426347	Fuel Feeding Mechanism
Sept. 16, 1947	No. 2427596	Burner for Solid Fuels
July 13, 1948	No. 2444985	Fuel Burner
Oct. 11, 1949	No. 2484161	Fuel Burners for Boilers
Jan. 31, 1950	No. 2496156	Rotary-type Burner for Solid Fuels

BIBLIOGRAPHY

Ancestry. "The Secret Weapon." November 29, 2011. www.ancestry.com.

Associated Press. "Europe Swarms with American Agents." *Journal and Tribune*, 1898, 1A.

Bergeron, Paul H. *Tennesseans and Their History.* 1st ed. Knoxville: University of Tennessee Press, 1999.

Berry, James, ed. *Convention of Weather Bureau Officials.* Washington, D.C: U.S. Department of Agriculture, 1898.

Brown, Fred. "Weston Fulton: Renowned American Entrepreneur with Strong County Down Connections." *Ulster-Scot*, February 2007, 15A.

Cunningham, Bob. "Inventor Whose Bombs Ruined U-Boats Has Friendly Visit in Hitler's Germany." *Knoxville News Sentinel*, October 12, 1934.

Day, Susan, and Randy Marion Quinn Fulton. E-mail message to Dewaine Speaks. June 18, 2013.

FlightSim. "Nightmares of a Forgotten War." November 21, 2011. www. FlightSim.com.

Fultonews. "Knoxville's Tom Edison." July 1980.

Fulton, William Frierson II. *Family Record and War Reminiscences.* Livingston, AL: Self-published, 1919.

History Rat. "Ronald Reagan and the Space Defense Initiative." January 16, 2010.

Hooper, Ed. *The "Can-Do" Company.* Images of America. Charleston, SC: Arcadia Publishing, 2003.

———. "Tennessee's Greatest Inventor." *Tennessee Star Journal*, February 19, 1999, 5A.

Knoxville Journal. "Fulton House Will Be Nurses Home." July 16, 1950.

———. "Knox Industrialist W.M. Fulton Dies." May 17, 1946.

———. "Mine Operator Buys Fulton Home." June 26, 1947.

———. "Mrs. Fulton, Widow of Inventor, Dies." November 11, 1971.

———. "Palatial Old Fulton Mansion to be Razed." August 22, 1967.

———. "Weston M. Fulton and Associates Purchase Plant of W.J. Savage Company; Consideration Is About $250,000." July 19, 1928.

———. "Weston Miller Fulton Obituary." May 18, 1946.

Knoxville News-Sentinel. "Fulton Residence." November 11, 1971.

———. "Weston Fulton, Knox Inventor, Dies at Home." May 16, 1946, 1A.

McNabb, William Ross. *Westcliff: Mr. Fulton's Mansion*. Knoxville: East Tennessee Historical Society, 1977.

Mellon, George, and J. Woolridge. *Standard History of Knoxville*. Chicago: Lewis Publishing Company, 1900.

Missile Threat. "Brilliant Pebbles." January 7, 2013.

Neely, Jack. *A History of the Most Democratic Place on Earth*. Knoxville, TN: Market Square District Association, 2009.

———. *Knoxville: This Obscure Prismatic City*. Charleston, SC: The History Press, 2009.

Romer, F. *This Expanding Age*. Knoxville, TN: n.p., 1928.

Shea, Patty, and Kim Cowart. "Talley Family Establishes Weston Miller Fulton Memorial Scholarship." *Tennessee Engineer*, fall 2005.

A State of Readiness. Knoxville, TN: Robertshaw Controls Company, June 1981.

Thomas, Ralph S. "The Story of Robertshaw Controls Company." Address to a National Newcomen Society dinner. Richmond, VA, November 6, 1974.

Ulster/Belfast News Letter. "Weston Fulton." March 31, 2007.

University Commons. "About the University Commons Retail Center." November 29, 2012.

U.S. Centennial of Flight Commission. "Norden Bombsight." November 22, 2011.

"Valuation of the Fulton Company." Historical material used in establishing a 1913 valuation by Mr. Fulton. Knoxville, TN, March 1, 1913.

Weals, Vic. "Fulton's Gadget Doomed Enemy Submarine Fleet." *Knoxville Journal*, April 8, 1982, 14A.

Wells, Earl. "An Evaluation of the Vocational Training Program at Fulton High School, 1956 Through 1960." Unpublished master's thesis, University of Tennessee, 1964.

Wikipedia. "Freedman's Bureau." www.wikipedia.org.

———. "Norden Bombsight." www.wikipedia.org.

———. "Phi Kappa Phi." www.wikipedia.org.

Williamson, Eva Avery, ed. *The Ancestors of Mary Helen Fulton Hartley.* Kenner, LA: n.p., February 6, 1977.

"Yours for Victory." Fulton Bellows Company advertisement.

ABOUT THE AUTHOR

Dewaine Speaks worked for the Fulton Sylphon Company for thirty-five years, ending his career there as national sales manager. He made sales calls and attended meetings with engineers in most states and several foreign countries. Some of the projects the company worked on while he was with the firm—most of which are described in this book—are listed below:

- Disney World monorail tire sensors
- automatic oxygen systems for airliners
- United States Gaseous Centrifuge Program
- dampening devices used in the transmissions of automobiles
- controls on the distiller at Jack Daniel's distillery
- automatic control of the Yugo automobile engine's air-fuel mixture
- bellows as part of the fuel control system for NASA rocket engines
- device that helps control the blood temperature of open-heart surgery patients
- automatic deployment of parachutes for pilots ejecting at high altitudes
- automobile thermostats for Nissan Motor Company
- system for providing water for astronauts in space
- Star Wars propulsion system

During his many meetings with engineers who had applications or problems to be solved, Speaks never failed to notice the respect that Fulton and his products received. He often wondered why Fulton's story had never been told. So, he set out to do just that.

Lightning Source UK Ltd.
Milton Keynes UK
UKHW010928011221
394888UK00003B/268

9 781540 250544